CREATIVITY
WITHOUT
FRONTIERS

Since the first human crawled deep into a cave to make art, creativity has flourished among rebels and risk takers, mavericks, and visionaries.

However, if creativity thrives among outsiders, how can it be nurtured inside large organizations? How can one build a team that works together to solve real problems while leaving room for individual inspiration? How can one ignite the creative spark without burning down the building?

Roy Sharples draws on decades of experience at the vanguard of business innovation and a deep affinity for applying an artistic instinct to explore these questions, offering novel solutions.

Contents

1 PHILOSOPHY IN THE BEDROOM
What creativity is, why it matters, and what difference it makes. Aspire to be as great as the things that are influencing you. Aim not to be like them, but to be as influential by defining your own unique structure and style. Constraints, barriers, principles, and standards are critical to expressing yourself through what you are, what you are not, and appreciating the differences.

2 THE MODERNISTS, MAVERICKS AND MISFITS
True artists are always outsiders looking in; rebels with a cause—themselves. They provide something new to the world that we live in, overturning the status quo by positively impacting people's lives and moving society forward. Learn how sustained creativity has always been a true differentiator. The people who transcend the status quo—and inspire others to do so, too—become our models for ingenuity.

3 POP CULTURE REFLECTS TIME
Learn how popular culture has mirrored time and change by connecting society, entertainment, politics, fashion, and technology by provoking action to change minds and translating experiences across space and time. Understand how to stand on the shoulders of giants by learning from history and how to avoid reinventing the wheel as you make progress in your creative pursuits.

4 CREATIVE SOCIETIES
Understand how societies are a catalyst for inspiring creativity and sociocultural movements, where people can realize their full potential and live more enriched, fulfilled, and happy lives.

5 CHAOS TO CULTURE
How to foster a culture of creativity through a do-it-yourself sensibility and a social system that allows people to create without fear and which is embraced, nurtured, imparted, and practiced by individuals, teams, and organizations; backed up with proven examples from creative industry experts.

Contents

1 PHILOSOPHY IN THE BEDROOM

PHILOSOPHY
IN THE
BEDROOM

What creativity is, why it matters, and what difference it makes. Aspire to be as great as the things that are influencing you. Aim not to be like them, but to be as influential by defining your own unique structure and style. Constraints, barriers, principles, and standards are critical to expressing yourself through what you are, what you are not, and appreciating the differences.

PHILOSOPHY IN THE BEDROOM

Creativity is the ability to make the invisible visible by taking what is not to create what is. It manifests what is inside you and around you by transcending the obvious, ordinary, and routine. It connects the past to the present by putting things together in new ways. Creativity is the belief in yourself and your ideas, always moving forward and never giving up!

True creatives are the outsiders looking in, the rebels with a cause. To be one, you must be comfortable taking a stand against oppressive forces and articulating your opinions and ideas without fear of retaliation. Creativity entails providing something new to the world, overturning the status quo by positively impacting people's lives, and helping society advance by making life more purposeful, engaging, and fulfilling. It also means embracing originality and making unique connections between disparate universes past and present to light the way into the future.

Creative people are people like you and me—ordinary people who do extraordinary things. The ability to be creative exists within everyone. It manifests itself in every domain and profession and at any age. You never lose the ability to be creative. In fact, I believe that creativity increases with time because we all gain more knowledge and insight as we experience more of life. Life events provide us with more reference points and the knowledge gained through experiencing them, combined with our imagination, maintains our childlike wonder throughout life. Insight truly knows no bounds. However, creativity does rely on intelligence to transform dreams and nascent ideas into things tangible and real.

PHILOSOPHY IN THE BEDROOM

This transformation infuses imagination, taste, style, and inherent messiness with an inner desperation and persistence, along with a desire to succeed that results in having the skill and practical know-how. To be creative, you must swim courageously against the tide in search of the authentic and new, while staving off false promises of easy gratification and immediate success in a world saturated with consumer-led celebrity culture, where everyone looks the same, and everything is for sale. Some of us must also transcend vermin-tongued conformists, separatist armchair analysts, and tiger parents—all of whom have the capacity to crush imaginations, inner voices, and dreams. This is the reality in which we live, and it is counter-intuitive to nurturing creativity.

However, curiously, it is hardship, melancholy, and adversity that often inspire creativity. People who survive alienation, oppression, poverty, and other life challenges realize that it fuels their genius when they are able to focus it. This primal desire to survive the odds with extraordinary intellectual ability, mental toughness, grit, and creative productivity is what fuels an insatiable drive for self-actualization. This, in turn, inspires creativity. And that is what this book is all about.

When you know how to channel your passion and energy into creativity and create meaningful outcomes, your outputs will be the next generation's inputs by lighting the way to the future and passing on the baton, leaving the world a better place. If you aspire to be as influential as the things that influence you—not to imitate them but to influence others in your own creative way—you can recreate the world.

PHILOSOPHY
IN THE
BEDROOM

By not letting your environment or anyone within it define you, you define your own purpose and mission. By this, I mean creating and adhering to your own personal constraints, barriers, principles, and standards to define yourself by what you are and what you are not and appreciate the difference. This means being acutely aware of your taste and emotions, which will free you to excel at your craft. This ensures that everything you dream about, make, and do is born of substance and integrity. When you are clear about yourself, you can guide your future and attract all the right people to your life and into your creative circle. Your goal is to become a model of true ingenuity, to be someone who regularly transcends the status quo and emboldens others to do the same.

Popular culture reflects life in time. It ignites societal change through a common set of practices, beliefs, and objects that encompass a shared meaning and social system that affects every aspect of life: art, design, music, film, fashion, television, literature, comics, brands, advertising, marketing, language, photography, politics, sports, food, how people look, talk, and act, and how these cultural products are branded, packaged, marketed to, and consumed by us. Popular culture influences our everyday lives and value systems, as well as our priorities and decisions. It ultimately fuels our creative influences and horsepower, both directly and indirectly.

Architecture and design influence how people feel, think and behave. It is a design and an expression that inspires a culture of creativity and allows people to interact in meaningful ways. Setting the right conditions, atmosphere, and environment inspires creativity, art, and beauty that people adapt and react to and reflect in their life and work. It affects how they view and interpret the world around them, their capacity to become self-actualized, and their ability to live fulfilled and happy lives.

PHILOSOPHY
IN THE
BEDROOM

Creativity expands the mind, broadens our perspectives, and helps us to eradicate prejudices. A creative society is one where we feel autonomous and free to express ourselves. Uniqueness, diversity, and self-expression are all acknowledged and celebrated through constructive support in developing our ideas. Society shapes who we are, just as our personal and collective identities shape society and future generations. People in teams and communities have a sense of belonging, which shapes our self-image by influencing how we see ourselves, how we interact with others, and how we respond to situations by trying out new ideas, experimenting with new ways of thinking and problem solving.

But if you are wondering how this all fits in with business, it's a logical progression, as the purpose of organizational development is to provide leading-edge thinking, practice, and programs. You cannot curate a culture of creativity by subscribing to it or buying it from a shelf, because it is a social system about values, skills, craftsmanship, and a way of doing that needs to be embraced and practiced throughout an organization to nurture people to create without fear.

My approach blends the art and science of the creative process: Dream, Make, and Do. The sequence is iterative and constant, and the alchemy lies in bringing it to life with purpose and impact. I have underpinned this by providing unique perspectives on creativity and the creative process from experts in the creative industry: actors, artists, art directors, branders, creative directors, curators, designers, educators, entrepreneurs, executives, filmmakers, illustrators, marketers, musicians, photographers, producers, and product developers.

PHILOSOPHY IN THE BEDROOM

You'll see how truly creative leaders broke the mold by making their own path to achieve mastery. Those who achieve greatness do not fit a formula or follow a structure. They follow their own path and manifest their inner feelings about the world by promoting their innate point of view and using their talent to craft poetry in a world where there is only prose; they grace the world with art.

To help you become an influential creative leader, I've established a Creative Excellence Model that details the collection of skills and competencies. These comprise principles that define what creative leaders must know and practice, and that holistically address leadership at the individual, team, and organizational levels. It is also relevant to and infuses the practices essential for all levels, from Fledglings to Journeymen, Experts to Innovators, and ultimately Artists. This model is based on my years of operating at the vanguard of building beloved brands, designing and bringing new products and services to market profitably, creating growth businesses globally, developing start-up businesses from the ground up, and leading multinational businesses and teams across 191 countries and forty-six languages.

I established and ran an independent record label and distribution company. I was a songwriter, musician, producer, artist, and maker who directed artistic practice and existential inspired ideologies into my work by pollinating across multiple domains and disciplines.

This book was created to fill the current void in the market: nothing quite like it exists. It is based upon my life experiences: what I've done, learned, observed, read, felt, listened to, where I've traveled and ventured, who I've collaborated and shared experiences with. It's built on my moral compass, and my natural

PHILOSOPHY
IN THE
BEDROOM

ability to take in and internalize information to fulfill my purpose in life. Finally, it's informed by how I've accomplished my goals to date.

I was born into and grew up in an environment that armed me with a strong work ethic and do-it-yourself sensibility, which contributed to my need for independence and self-dependence at a young age. I looked and felt different, which propelled my natural instinct to be a lone wolf and to continuously swim against the tide of growing up in Caledonia's northeastern peninsula's bitter edge. A strong aesthetic orientation, an eye for well-designed things, a commitment to making sacrifices, mental toughness, persistence, and the independence to follow my impulse to create all triggered my imagination. I believe nothing is worth doing in life that involves ordinariness and repetition. I gravitated toward metropolitan spaces to express myself. I resided in four different countries to embrace diversity and difference, and learned the skills that I needed, doing so in my own style and at my own pace to love and live a fulfilled and happy life.

PHILOSOPHY IN THE BEDROOM

My philosophy is never to be another brick in the wall. Be in the moment, push forward for the greater good with true grit, for the sake of your beliefs, your commitments, and for others. I've learned to lead by example, be mission-driven and agile, adapt to different styles, continuously learn, innovate, truly care, and never waste a minute. After all, the most used noun in the English language is time, and I want to make the most of it. I believe in karma—justice is my golden rule—and in living life guided by my passions, with a positive and progressive attitude, being authentic and true to myself. I believe in cultivating lifelong relationships and partnerships grounded in trust, honesty, and transparency. I've constantly infused this into everything I stand for, what I do, and how I do it. I blend art and science seamlessly into my craft and gravitate toward the unknown in its original state of existence as an entrepreneur, executive, engineer, marketer, artist, and maker. I've infused these experiences and insights within this book to help unlock your creative potential.

PHILOSOPHY IN THE BEDROOM

Now is the time for you to define and bring to life your own authentic manifesto. The defining question is a stalemate: should you be acceptable to others or to yourself? Learn how to reject conventional perceptions and the restrictions imposed on you by unlocking your true creative potential. Set yourself free by finding your unique philosophy and true self with a deep search into your most personal space: the bedroom of your mind's landscape, where your most rudimentary art originated with its tail trapped in the door desperately trying to get out like a tortured spirit crushed in the red light of life. Then get ready to redefine your future.

THE
MODERNISTS
MAVERICKS
& MISFITS

THE
MODERNISTS, MAVERICKS AND MISFITS

True artists are always outsiders looking in; rebels with a cause—themselves. They provide something new to the world that we live in, overturning the status quo by positively impacting people's lives and moving society forward. Learn how sustained creativity has always been a true differentiator. The people who transcend the status quo—and inspire others to do so, too—become our models for ingenuity.

THE MODERNISTS, MAVERICKS AND MISFITS

The modernists, mavericks, and misfits are the real iconoclasts when it comes to being authentically creative. These restless natives are the outsiders who never seem to quite fit in. I think of them as rebels with a cause. They are the real deal in that they are the self-defined, self-styled, self-educated, would-be cultured agitators who overturn the status quo by rejecting conventions and creating the new and modern—much like an artist creating a work of art. But their canvas is in creating innovative ideas that define new cultures and worlds, by leapfrogging over their respective peers and industry. They have the ability to see the future, finding solutions to problems before others even know they exist. This creative way of thinking is integral to modernizing and reinventing old ways of doing things with original and often groundbreaking perspectives that are keys to business success and important in moving society forward. This aspect of creativity means rejecting convention and challenging the status quo in everyday life. By continually analyzing and questioning, you can lead creatively and provoke actions that bring about change. Looking back in history, we see people of action who inspire others to follow them by example. As others take notice of a successful leader's creative sensibility, they begin their own self-discovery process. This is how creatives move society forward.

If you want to join the truly creative ranks, you owe it to yourself to be willing to color outside the lines and put your creative ideas to work, knowing that some will succeed while others may fail.

THE MODERNISTS, MAVERICKS AND MISFITS

People who achieve greatness do not fit a formula or follow a structure. They break the mold by charting their own, sometimes unorthodox, path. You'll be able to tap into your creativity if you have no trouble turning left when told to turn right, breaking through the doors that you're not supposed to enter, or even knock on, and fighting your way toward making your unique voice heard and your original style noticed by driving your actions forward. This is what is meant by seeing the previously unseen. The ability to challenge conventional tastes and perceptions and persist in being diametrically opposed to the values perceived as the norm is your power. So, tap into your primal need to discover and innovate for the greater good and a better world by being in control of your art. Do not compromise your integrity. Circumnavigate the mainstream so you can develop a deeper relationship with your audience. Be present, live in the moment, and stay true to yourself. It is about your attitude, imagination, and execution.

SEEING THE
UNSEEN

Art has the power to transcend into revelation and transform us from our default mode of what we see and feel. Once that happens, we don't look at things the same way again because we are given a new sight: insight! David Bowie, a true creative if ever there was one, spoke and lived by his own words: "Tomorrow belongs to those who can hear it coming."

Bowie had the uncanny ability to foresee future trends in music and fashion—and indeed in anything he set his mind to—and he used this knack to tilt popular culture. Bowie was the original "influencer". He accurately predicted the impact of the Internet in the interview David Bowie speaks to Jeremy Paxman on BBC Newsnight in 1999, when he eloquently praised the nascent technology by saying, "[It] carries the flag of being subversive and possibly rebellious, and chaotic, and nihilistic."

Bowie was able to envision what the Internet would do to transform the way music gets made by artists and experienced by audiences, against resistance from music industry insiders who—fearing the unknown—dissed the Internet. Bowie went full out and embraced it; "It's becoming more about the audience," he said. "So, from my standpoint, being an artist, I'd like to see what the new construction is between artist and audience. There is a breakdown."

Bowie was able to see the unseen, beyond his time. Using new internet services seemed farfetched for artists, but what he predicted became the norm. Musicians now make music, perform live, and engage with fans online, making it accessible, affordable, and convenient to experience music from anywhere at any time.

SEEING THE
UNSEEN

How many times have you proclaimed, "I could have done that"? Yes, we have all come across something so banal and bereft of sophistication that there is no doubt that we could have done it just as well or better. But, as the saying goes, "hindsight is 20/20". The key to creativity is being able to perceive and understand the context of something new, perhaps an invention, and how it will be used in the future. Most people tend to judge something in the present by its complexity, production value, and acceptability, when its true value may lie in the future.

Using real-life, social issues, and images as a source of subject matter, artists experiment and innovate to accurately capture society as they believe it exists—diametrically opposing prior art movements that idealized their reality. Modernists like Salvador Dali, Henri Matisse, Pablo Picasso, and Andy Warhol were central to the modern art movement. In the 1990s, Banksy continued this sensibility by cultivating satirical street art and subversive epigrams that combined dark sarcasm with war critiques, and political and anti-capitalist messages in a distinct stenciling technique, ultimately moving outlawed street art into the mainstream media.

Surrealist artist Salvador Dalí claimed that his images were "dream sequences" inspired by his subconscious, which attempted to create art that was "truer" than life by avoiding logic, which he believed got in the way of his imagination.

SEEING THE
UNSEEN

Such true innovators see their audience's very soul via intuition and empirical, observational, and anecdotal methods. They are people of action who are always future-oriented. They are the doers—the people who start things, move the world forward, and inspire others. Breaking boundaries is part of their daily routine.

Purpose and passion drive innovators to improve the world. In the pursuit of greatness, remember that you don't need permission from anyone, in the spirit of Muhammad Ali; "impossible is nothing"!

He was a beacon and signpost for change who shook society up, especially in America during the civil rights movement, rejecting what he termed his slave name, Cassius Clay, converting to Islam and refusing military service to go at war with Vietnam. A sacrifice that cost him the heavyweight championship and a ban from boxing at the pinnacle of his career.

During a conservative time in history, these were courageous actions to take a moral stand that helped push society forward. Even after Ali's organs had stopped, laid to rest on his deathbed, his heart continued to beat for another thirty minutes, which is scientifically unheard of and a further justification that the heart is the soul!

RESTLESS
NATIVES

Musician, singer, and songwriter Johnny Marr nailed it when he said that the music industry had never created anything in its history! This statement was published in the UK's *The Independent* newspaper in November 2008 in an article titled "The outsiders: misfits and mavericks who make music magical".

The music industry has arguably never really invented anything within itself. It has brought many talented pioneers to life and helped make and market groundbreaking records and musical events. But the reality is that music business insiders haven't created anything themselves that has truly stood the test of time.

Musical innovations always come from outsiders and mavericks, such as Robert Johnson, Howlin' Wolf, Muddy Waters, Elvis Presley, Little Richard, Bob Dylan, Jimi Hendrix, Patti Smith, Joni Mitchell, and groups like The Beatles, The Rolling Stones, The Doors, The Velvet Underground, Talking Heads, The Sex Pistols, The Smiths, and Kraftwerk.

Marr continues, "They created their vehicle and drove it ahead of the music industry and, in doing so, they created their market. They did their research, development, and self-marketing out of necessity, rejection, frustration, talent, and vision. They did it, and they still do it, in small clubs, playing in front of a few people, supporting other bands, going up and down the country in little vans, they do it in homemade studios, they do it on social media. They don't do it on The X Factor or America's Got Talent. They are always people from the outside!"

Transfer this paradigm to the rest of the arts, business, politics, and society, and you can easily see that the motto and model are the same. Many innovators are classic outsiders who disrupted, invented, and changed the faces of their industries forever.

RESTLESS
NATIVES

Andrew Carnegie, Walt Disney, Henry Ford, Steve Jobs, Elon Musk, Nikola Tesla, and the Wright Brothers rose from obscurity to radically transform industry and how people lived.

Often, by accident, disruption can have a domino effect outside the intentional target and area of expertise. For example, Apple's iTunes became a multimedia content and hardware synchronization management system and e-commerce platform; it was originally envisioned as a music player. It ended up disrupting the music industry by providing consumers with the ability to legally buy only the songs they wanted to hear at a significantly lower cost than on other platforms. Another example is Coca-Cola, which was first invented by pharmacist John Stith Pemberton to cure headaches before becoming a household name.

This is like Outsider Art, where the actual art is produced by self-taught artists with no formal training, who can often have a naïve quality because they have not trained as artists or worked within the conventional art production structures. They do not follow a conventional path, structure, or formula. They follow their instinct and define their own structure and style. Sometimes, the farther you are from a problem, the more likely you will find a solution because you can see the situation from a fresh perspective and often apply novel solutions to a disparate field.

Do you remember the last time you were bored—experiencing true, unfathomable boredom where you stepped away from the distractions of any technologies long enough to feel bored? Do you recall not having an iPhone, social media, apps, the Internet, or games to pass the time? It's tough to be bored in a world that is increasingly consumed with technology and where social media is in overdrive, constantly available at our fingertips 24/7.

RESTLESS
NATIVES

Being in a temporary state of boredom can trigger your imagination to unlock new opportunities and experiences. Boredom can inspire you to seek disruptive ways, including being altruistic and empathetic and engaging in prosocial tasks.

Conceptual artist Linder Sterling said in an interview 'I have a library of every perversion on the planet' in *The Guardian* newspaper in October 2015, "Punk at its purest came and went very quickly, in the blink of history's eye. Great creativity can come out of boredom, and I think that's what the younger generation miss. Boredom was punk's seedbed, and social media does all it can to eliminate the void. But I hope that a very bored teenager in a bedroom on the outskirts of Hull will one day smash their iPhone against the wall and reinvent punk."

Social media has helped many organizations get off the ground by providing them with a vehicle to grow and promote themselves at an unprecedented scale, connect with people, and communicate globally, regardless of geography or language. That said, it has had a detrimental impact by being an enabler that fuels mental health issues, destabilizes emotions, consumes and wastes energy and time, and distracts people from living full, enriched lives.

Linder's point was that social media and the Internet have saturated our daily lives. Our brains are overloaded with information and distractions, so we aren't using our imaginations to disrupt and start a revolution. We're quickly satiated because we can simply move from one thing to the other. Being bored for a while can rest our brains and better equip us to solve problems afterward by revitalizing our taste and primal need for adventure or discovering the next thing. Our newly rested and energized brains can revolt against the banal and find new alternatives.

Creativity is
fearlessly leading
without frontiers by
creating something
new that moves the
world forward

DREAM
Imagine the impossible
by making the invisible
visible

CREATIVITY

DO
Produce solutions
that add commercial
and societal value

Creativity is the
ability to make the
invisible visible by
taking what is not
to create what is

MAKE
Take what is not and make
it what is by applying a Do-
It-Yourself sensibility to
create and craft

The poles of innovation

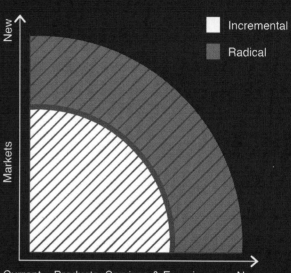

Nothing survives long term without embracing both radical innovation and incremental innovation.

Every successful movement, organization, or team needs to continuously innovate or they will be surpassed by competition in the longer term.

They key is to maintain a balance between the two poles of innovation.

THE POLES OF
INNOVATION

Understanding history is important to architects, artists, designers, filmmakers, musicians, writers, and other creators. Instead of needlessly reinventing the wheel, historical knowledge provides insight for authentic creativity and accelerates real innovation to gain a significant competitive advantage by leapfrogging over contemporaries.

Few movements survive long-term without embracing both radical and incremental innovation. Every successful artist, entrepreneur, and business needs to innovate continuously or risk being surpassed by competition in the longer term.

Radical innovation introduces a new business model and way of doing, where its invention dismantles and surpasses an existing business model and the status quo that surrounds it. In the business continuum, it typically equates to higher risks, but can offer higher returns. It requires the ability to envision and treat failure as a step forward, not a step backward or a reason to disengage. Startups are typically biased toward radical innovation by having significantly fewer constraints than larger organizations. They can afford to take greater risks, focus on the bigger picture, have more inspirational objectives, and be willing to experiment, reimagine, and design for the new with fewer inhibitors.

THE POLES OF
INNOVATION

Apple experimented with the music application iTunes. It realized there was no quality MP3 player on the market, so it created its own, the iPod. Eventually, it dematerialized its own technology by pivoting into another adjacent market, smartphones, with the iPhone! This led to Apple revolutionizing both the music and telecommunications industries. If that wasn't enough, it reinvented itself from being a personal computing company to an all-encompassing consumer electronics, computer software, and online services global leader. The Tesla Powerwall disrupted energy storage by using the technology that Tesla developed for its cars to branch into this new billion-dollar market. Amazon pivoted from selling physical books to being a global marketplace for e-books and e-readers. Netflix transitioned from mailing DVDs to video streaming over the web. Uber disrupted food delivery with online ordering. The camera company Fujifilm is disrupting cosmetics since the thousands of chemicals used in Fujifilm's core business were identified as antioxidants that can be used for cosmetic purposes.

Randomness can be a trigger to making radical innovation happen. For example, Google's search business depends upon large numbers of people seeking information on the web, which is informed by their previous viewings, predicting that humans follow similar paths. Achieved by creating algorithms for page ranking where a series of steps are sequenced where the next step is random yet informed by the previous step. As the sequence moves forward, the contents of the present state change, which increases the relevance of the content and the diversity of the input, accumulating and storing up knowledge in their memory as they interact more in their social networks. The more interactions and diverse the input, the likelihood of radical ideas and innovation.

THE POLES OF
INNOVATION

Incremental innovation is a series of small improvements made to an existing business model, product, service, or experience to achieve the desired business goal and differentiate from the competition by building on current value propositions and offerings. Mature businesses tend to be biased toward innovating incrementally to maintain their existing customers' needs and grow their customer base in a risk-mitigated and tangible way. Typically characterized by narrower objectives and quantitative goals, they also take advantage of market research, focus groups, and prototyping. These large organizations focus on continuous improvement. They work toward defined milestones and rely upon internal sources of information to fill knowledge gaps.

Companies like Disney and Coca-Cola have mastered the art and science of relevance and customer retention by incrementally innovating extensions to their product offerings through product enhancements, acquisition, and experiential branding. This has enabled them to stay relevant, tap into emerging trends, and continually bring something new to customers while remaining the market leaders.

When economic growth is declining, organizations are forced to make tough decisions about prioritizing what to invest in and how they should manage costs; They focus on efficiency rather than innovation and long-term growth. This continuum needs a balanced approach to managing the risk of cost and efficiency with long-term innovation and growth. History tells us that in times of economic adversity, the phoenix is ripe to rise from the ashes, as we have learned from Microsoft, Facebook, Pinterest, Netflix, Uber, and Airbnb—all born in a recession. This is because it is a time that tends to embrace new ways of doing things that provide solutions to problems in a more cost-efficient and effective manner.

ECONOMICS OF EVERYDAY LIFE

People can get used to things quickly. When you first arrive somewhere, you tend to notice all the little details that make up the impression of the experience, such as the architecture, the sky's color, car design, food, fashion, the way people look and dress, and the smell of life. As you get used to the new place, you usually don't notice these things anymore.

In economics, we discuss "diminishing marginal returns". The taste of your first chocolate bar is savored and cherished. The second bar still tastes good, but not as good. Then you eat the third one and realize that you've had enough. The desire to eat any more chocolate bars is gone.

So, unless you can continuously innovate and provide differentiated or continually improved products, services, or experiences that delight consumers, they will soon become uninterested and go elsewhere for the next best thing to fulfill their desires.

Sustaining innovation means institutionalizing it as part of your team or organization's culture. Continuously deliver end-to-end design through audience advocacy, new ideas, and end-to-end thinking. Seek insight from your audience by getting data that will help you understand their primary needs, concerns, highest priorities, key expectations, and the most significant market trends. Use this valuable input to guide your approach to your product development or quality improvements. Never forget that every single object we see and touch was once an idea inside someone's head. The key is to turn your ideas into outcomes that have value.

EMPIRES
AND EGOS

The bottom line is that all commercial businesses exist to make money. Creating business value requires understanding what drives a company to operate and be successful: asset efficiency, operating margin, option value, and revenue growth. The key is to act in ways that drive sustained business value by prioritizing and executing the right strategies and tactics in an adaptive and scalable way.

Pure and simple, right?

Then you put people into the mix, and it gets murky. The probability of success and failure oscillates wildly because it is ultimately all about people and execution.

When you have more than one person, there is politics. When people assess their well-being by their own ego, they can become self-fulfilling, critical, judgmental, cunning, manipulative of others, rigid, and inflexible. The constant need for praise and approval and feeling superior to everyone becomes increasingly apparent. This state of mind can be counter-productive to progress and reverse any good you do, leading to mistrust, dysfunctionality, and toxicity. People organized in teams and corporate structures are rational. They are self-contained economic engines applying their brand of rationality to situations; "What is in it for me?" because people, by nature, tend to make decisions based on the benefit to them.

EMPIRES
AND EGOS

Put simply by author Robin Farmer in "Farmer's Law", "the greater the degree of governance, the lesser the degree of innovation". Depending on the business's nature, the management system will either be ingrained in the whole organization's DNA or developed. "Governance is a by-product of success, and control is the natural requirement of an executive. Balancing governance against the desire for innovation can be achieved but has to be agreed upon from top to bottom." Understanding the risks of relaxing governance or investing with a venture capital mentality is crucial in this sense.

Teams and organizations must develop the process and infrastructure to promote, enable, incentivize, and facilitate creativity and imagination. Otherwise, the organization is likely to witness lost opportunities through the lack of a framework or process to capture, ideate, and realize great ideas. This process involves breaking down decaying organizational silos from rigid functional and operational structures and building highly skilled, focused, and agile multidisciplinary venture-like teams, which gravitate toward a shared sense of purpose, curiosity, and the greater good.

Jacques Nasser was the CEO of Ford from 1999 to 2001. At the beginning of his helm, he led Ford to be the world's most profitable automaker, with profits over $7 billion, which made him golden and liberated him to experiment and innovate.

EMPIRES
AND EGOS

Jacques believed that Ford could not compete across the entire automotive market, including the luxury car space. For that purpose, he formed the Premier Automotive Group that consisted of Aston Martin, Jaguar Land Rover, Volvo, Mazda, Mercury, and Lincoln. This gave him the space and focus to dream up a vision to transform Ford from being an automaker to a consumer business. He sought to acquire the automotive ecosystem to have an integrated end-to-end distribution operation and supply chain system experience.

His ambitious transformation enabled consumers to self-select the car they wanted and customize it online, then have it built and delivered to them within 14 days. He also diversified Ford's business to encompass e-commerce, car distribution, auto repair shops, and junkyards.

Although the vision was compelling, the timing to realize it was not. Within a highly governed, complacent, and monolithic dinosaur industry, the inability to accelerate the change needed to realize the vision, combined with terrible luck, was the inhibitor that would stop the revolution. Arguably, some of this was out of Jacque's control, such as the Ford Explorer's product recalls, due to faulty Firestone tires that Ford ultimately lost the legal case on. They ended up having to fund the expense out of their own pocket, faced multiple other friction points internally and within the industry, and struggled through the auto industry's nosedive. All of these forces not only inhibited the vision but ultimately led to Jacque's departure.

His vision was premature, especially in comparison to Elon Musk's, which was timely and benefitted from having the right talent, agility, and resources.

THE MACHINE THAT CHANGED THE WORLD

Industrialization transformed the world's collective production from agricultural work, predominantly done by humans, to goods manufacture, predominantly mechanized mass production. People were replaced by assembly lines to improve operating efficiency and increase production speed in a predictable, scalable, and cost-effective way. The industrializing of a business at scale is about mitigating uncertainty, ambiguity, and judgment and creating a fine-tuned formula of simple blocks that anyone can use. It also involves defining all production processes, training people on using them, locking them, and allowing zero deviation.

If you can use a machine to prevent human error, do so. Use devices for efficiency and predictability, but never in your interaction with clients; people should deal with fellow people, not bots. You also need to define the ideal customer experience—not the process, but the customer experience itself.

Starbucks, McDonald's, and many fast food, retail, manufacturing, corporate media, and entertainment companies' business models are based on these industrialized mass-produced and mass-consumed products where one size fundamentally fits all.

This equates to the obsessive watching of televised, karaoke-culture, "Celebration of Specialness" competitions that has sunk our sophisticated tastes and imagination to the likes of American Idol and Pop Idol reality contests.

THE MACHINE THAT CHANGED THE WORLD

Productize, formalize, and automate the whole lot as much as possible, whether in toolsets, models, or prescriptive outcomes.

This means creating everything by the same common standard and means, often with banal results. This is an application of science for mass-produced products, and is scalable and predictable. It is not art for the masses, nor does it provide customized people-centric solutions. It is a one size fits all product push model. Hire people who will follow these rules. Improve things as you and your employees learn. Don't ever deviate from the process—improve it. Challenge those who differ—through justification or reasoning—and never forget that innovation is essential within the frame. Eliminate disruptions. Promote employees who improve on processes. Keep reviewing your framework by creating a continuous improvement process and loop.

These organizations and their business models are designed for scale with a focus on process repetition and efficiency. Predictability and producing at a fast pace are the game's name as the formula to dominate their respective industry and market. This restricts consumer choice and results in higher prices than in a more competitive market situation. This is the decaying cornerstone of how monolithic companies built their business system, where standardized one size fits all products were manufactured using assembly lines, automated robotic machines, and human labor.

Shifts in consumer needs require mass customization, which is driven by market pull rather than purely product push factors, and products and services made and marketed by combining the personalization of built-to-order products with low unit costs. The consumer should always be at the center of the design.

DEADLY
SINS

Art invents. Science evolves. Technologies improve. Industries change. Economics and politics adapt. Society moves forward. Human life goes on. We exist in time, where change is constant.

To adapt, grow, and flourish you need to keep your finger on the pulse of your market's ever-evolving needs and preferences so that you can make changes to your approach. The golden rule is to avoid the deadly sin of complacency and greed kicking in like a debt that you can't cure—don't take the cowardly way and cave in. Instead, stand unshakingly aware and resilient by constantly evolving and innovating!

Why? In general, people can be shiftless and self-gratifying, and as a result, the future will leave them behind. This is because they can self-destruct through excess and become victims of their own success by cultivating destructive habits and complacency.

Avoid at all costs falling asleep at the wheel, getting permanently drunk on your own Kool-Aid, surrounding yourself with b and c players, getting lazy and fat, where you can't see the wood for the trees and all the beast of prey, and making ego-based decisions.

DEADLY
SINS

According to Steve Jobs, "Xerox could have owned the entire computer industry, could have been the IBM of the nineties, could have been the Microsoft of the nineties." Xerox missed the opportunity due to its self-inflicted fixed mindset curtailed its ability to grow and evolve due to its inability to commercialize its products. Kodak's complacency from its dominance of the traditional photography market led to it missing the shift to online photo sharing. BlackBerry sank from owning over half of the American and a fifth of the global smartphone market to zero. Blockbuster monopolized the video rental market until Netflix disrupted it by adapting to customer needs and technological changes. The learnings are to have an effective strategy with a clear value proposition, adapt to market changes agilely, and rigorous execution at speed.

It is exactly the same in the creative arts. Its why art movements come and go, fashions flash and burn. Recycle! Repackage! Reissue! Re-evaluate the painting, song, film, show, performance, event, and satiate the audience. This is the lazy and habitual nature of human beings. We get consumed easily and bored quickly, and our minds just simply are not big enough to consume and look beyond north, south, west, and east, 24/7, 365 days per year.

Effective prioritization, being laser focused, and disciplined execution are the keys to success. It is just as important to decide what you do not do as it is what you do.

TECHNOLOGY
OVERDRIVE

Particularly in the Western world, most people have access to everything that is produced today. The digital revolution has democratized information and accelerated the pace of change. It is a world that is increasingly technology-mediated, changing how we live, learn, work, get things done, and blur the boundaries between physical and virtual life.

Products are constantly being connected to real-world experiences in virtual environments. Society is becoming more augmented by interactive digital content and information.

An extensive catalog of music is instantly available. We have access to many of the movies made since the beginning of cinema. We can watch them and play games online, and interact in real-time despite geographic differences.

Social media has had an omnipresent impact on people. Facebook, Instagram, Twitter, YouTube, and LinkedIn have become the fabric of our lives, allowing people to share stories about their everyday experiences and build their personal brand around their passions, beliefs, and activities. Since learning how to use the Internet in the 1990s, we've evolved and internalized it by making it part of our social routine.

Numerous industries and professions have been disrupted, reimagined, reinvented, or abandoned. Take journalism as one example; it has seen a rapid move to "media by the masses" by having countless contributions from non-journalists. One regularly reads the social reviews and commentary rather than the story itself. Who's in control now, and who is actually the journalist?

TECHNOLOGY
OVERDRIVE

The blurring of physical and virtual presence continues to drive us toward an existence where the edges will no longer be the boundaries. We have become increasingly driven by our primal need to be social, by our need for social recognition and celebration, and by our insatiable curiosity about authentic content and insights.

The Harvard Business Review published in July 2017, "Digital Transformation Is Racing Ahead and No Industry Is Immune". The article claimed, "Research shows that since 2000, 52% of companies in the Fortune 500 have either gone bankrupt, been acquired, or ceased to exist as a result of digital disruption. The collision of the physical and digital worlds has affected every dimension of society, commerce, enterprises, and individuals." While many factors have contributed to these organizations' rise and fall, no one is immune!

People were once judged fairly and squarely on their musical tastes. Your personal music collection was your private medical record. Going to my local independent record store each Saturday was a religious pilgrimage. As an ardent record collector, it was a magical experience to immerse myself in the romance and divine luxury of the sight, touch, and smell of the circular polyvinyl chloride disks, physically representing each audio waveform groove cut of the original recording, categorically obsessing over the sleeves to discover who the artists involved were, what the lyrics were and what they meant, where the records were made, who produced them, and who crafted the artwork. Every aspect of the record was a work of art.

TECHNOLOGY
OVERDRIVE

Discovering them was an obsessive and romantic experience. Then, the economics of everyday life united, took over, and dropped the bankruptcy atom bomb through growing competition from mass discounters and Internet piracy, combined with technology innovations from the pirates of Silicon Valley. Apple and Spotify changed the way we purchase and consume music through digital streaming. Traditional record companies failed to adapt to the digital revolution. Companies like Apple cleaned up shop and took over the market by becoming the legal online market leader through their iTunes download service that provides access to millions of songs for a monthly subscription fee.

The impact of technological disruption in the creative industries alone has been profound. Technologies like artificial intelligence, blockchain, augmented and virtual reality are reshaping how we live and work, art, filmmaking, journalism, music, photography, production, and more. Television distribution has been overturned by digital distribution platforms such as Netflix and Hulu. In the music industry, Apple, Amazon, and Spotify have provided more convenient, accessible, and affordable solutions for consumers to stream music on-demand. Wikipedia has replaced the encyclopedia. Online bookstores have forced brick-and-mortar stores into extinction. Self-publishing online has outfoxed publishers and printers. Apple Pay and PayPal are dominating online banking to the point where physical cash has become irrelevant. Uber and Lyft offer alternative taxis and private transportation services by providing passengers with the convenience of requesting and paying for rides through their phones. In some scenarios, Airbnb has made home rental more attractive than the traditional hotels and motels. And industrial robots have largely displaced assembly line workers.

TECHNOLOGY
OVERDRIVE

Henry Ford revolutionized the automotive industry by making the assembly line produce affordable cars for the masses, which changed society and how we lived and worked by making it quicker and more convenient to get around. This helped the economy prosper by giving birth to many businesses and spin-off industries, which created thousands of new jobs. Fast forward to the current day, where Tesla has manufactured battery packs at an affordable price for mass-market consumption to make sustainable transportation a reality. If research comes to fruition, over half the cars in the next 20–30 years will be electric and will disrupt and significantly reduce the need for oil. As we envision the future car, the signposts point toward electric, autonomous, and connected vehicles empathetic to society's needs, offering us improved safety, less pollution, more time, and customized services and experiences through intelligent technologies.

Technological advancement and innovation are important to society's evolution. They enable novel products, services, and experiences to create new opportunities and improve our lives and living standards, improving our productivity by affecting how we communicate, learn, and interact in our everyday lives.

How soon is the future? One thing for sure is the future is unwritten, and everything is possible!

3 POP CULTURE REFLECTS TIME

POP CULTURE REFLECTS TIME

Learn how popular culture has mirrored time and change by connecting society, entertainment, politics, fashion, and technology by provoking action to change minds and translating experiences across space and time. Understand how to stand on the shoulders of giants by learning from history and how to avoid reinventing the wheel as you make progress in your creative pursuits.

POP CULTURE
REFLECTS
TIME

History helps us understand the world, cultures, events, and change by providing invaluable stories, lessons, and philosophies from which we learn. The past has made us who we are today. Understanding history builds better connections and broadens our capacity by allowing us to stand on the shoulders of giants. We learn from them and build on their innovations. History educates us on how society, technology, and government worked in the past to better understand how we got to the present day and how it works now. It arms us with the insights to create a better way forward.

We all exist in time, which is a progression from the past into the future, moving in one direction. Design influences society by communicating through visual, word, and sonic, changing opinions, instilling values, and translating experiences to people across space and time. It is an expression of the soul that experiences ideas and provides us with purpose and meaning. Design is a vehicle for time and social change that interconnects society, entertainment, politics, fashion, and technology, which translates into popular culture—practices, beliefs, and rituals prevalent in society at any given point in time.

Popular culture expresses society's shared experiences and is a function of what society consumes through entertainment, fashion, politics, and technology. As soon as we enter the planet, we are immersed in popular culture influencing us through the toys and games we play with, media programs we watch, brands, advertisements, and products we consume, the music we listen to, the art we make, books and comics we read, and the clothes we wear.

POP CULTURE
REFLECTS
TIME

This reflects the moment in time, life in motion, and contributes to society's evolution by teaching us something new. It challenges us to critically consider the society we live in and empathize, by recognizing ourselves in each other and bridging our differences through providing us with a similarity of spirit and sense of community.

While time is constant, events can be cyclical within time, regurgitating the past within the present. For example, the children of the 1970s were born to baby boomers, leading to their influence in specific product lines; fashion, music, art, cartoons, video games, toys, and the like. These children grew up, entered the workforce, and became creators, infusing their creations with the qualities they loved. Similarly, adaptations in literature can reflect the culture and society of the period in which they were set and help shape the future's learnings and culture.

Kate Newell is Dean of the School of Liberal Arts at the Savannah College of Art and Design. Her research includes adaptation and intersections of literature and visual culture. She is the author of *Expanding Adaptation Networks: From Illustration to Novelization*.

To discover how the adaptation of visual culture works beyond just TV and film, expanding into genres such as mobile apps, video games, interactive media, and the avant-garde, Kate wrote, "I look at all types of paper-based adaptations, including illustration, novelization, literary maps, and pop-up books to track how an originally produced work in one medium has been adapted multiple times, across multiple media and platforms to understand how that process and the journey of that adaptation shapes the cultural understanding of that work."

POP CULTURE REFLECTS TIME

She continued, "When we think about the many different adaptations of Robert Louis Stevenson's *Dr. Jekyll and Mr. Hyde,* he doesn't describe Mr. Hyde's character in any depth, other than vaguely defined characteristics. However, the adaptations solidify the complexity of his character. By the time he is characterized in Alan Moore's *The League of Extraordinary Gentlemen*, he's become a secretive, mysterious, and violent man-beast hulk. They are all linked as cultural productions across all these adaptations – yet none are the definitive source text that adds up, even though we might think of the novel as the source being drawn from, from works that came before it, and newspaper accounts that came before from other productions that came before. It's all of these many different forms of adaptation, both big and small, that contribute to what our culture understands as a given work of art."

This is a chronological view of the last seventy years, since the birth of rock 'n' roll, of some of the key events in popular culture that have affected society and the interaction between people in their everyday lives.

Popular culture timeline

Time the traveler

1950s

Comics captured the imagination. Rock 'n' roll encouraged rebellion. Television sharpened the mind.

1960s

Bell-bottoms, long hair, love, experimentation with psychedelic experiences, anarchy, and revolution were memorable trends and occurrences.

1970s

Rapid pace of societal change, egalitarian society, diversity, broad-ranging styles, and tastes.

1980s

Self-centered, materialistic, androgynous, and money-making time; a decade that witnessed the rise of consumer goods.

1990s

Multiculturalism, alternative media, grunge, rave, hip hop, cable television, and the Internet marked this decade.

2000s

Growth of the Internet, excessive access to information, mass globalization, the expansion of the service industry, and the rise of online platforms.

2010s

Blurring of virtual and physical life. Edges were no longer the boundaries. Intelligent machines emerged.

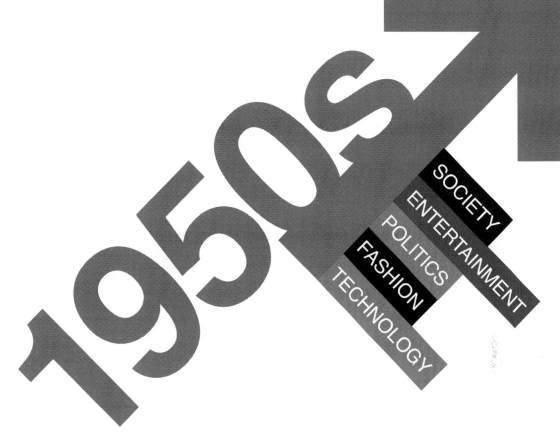

1950s

SOCIETY
ENTERTAINMENT
POLITICS
FASHION
TECHNOLOGY

Society
Television revolutionized the way people saw themselves and the world around them. With the economy booming after World War II and low unemployment rates, families had disposable income to afford consumer goods, houses and cars which catalyzed an urban to suburban migration. Multiple art movements started, such as; abstract expressionism, neo-dada, and pop art.

Entertainment
The decade experienced the globalization of pop music, as personified by Elvis Presley, rock 'n' roll, country, rhythm and blues, gospel, country and western, and actors like Marlon Brando, Marilyn Monroe, and James Dean who reflected youth culture's desire to rebel against adult authority. Movies and television entertained while buttressing conformity to societal norms, patriotism, and religious faith.

Politics
The Cold War continued between the United States and the Soviet Union. The civil rights movement started to push for equal rights for all Americans.

Fashion
Clear gender divide. Men wore casual day-to-day style, leather jackets, and slicked, greased hair. Women wore elegant, and formal attire, with matched accessories. Bouffant, duck tail, pompadour, pony tails, poodle cut, thick fringe, short and curly hairstyles.

Technology
Rapid advancement in mass communication. Television disrupted radio; magazines and newspapers were the primary sources of information.

1960s

SOCIETY
ENTERTAINMENT
POLITICS
FASHION
TECHNOLOGY

Society

A decade of hope, change, and war drove significant societal change. Protest manifested through multiple influential activists and social movements that changed people's lives and made societies more inclusive and progressive.

Entertainment

Movies tackled social anathemas, such as violence and sex, triggering appeal and debate. The Beatles changed pop music forever, as did The British Invasion, folk-rock, hard rock, Motown, psychedelic rock, protest music, roots rock, and surf rock.

Politics

The Civil rights protests and the Vietnam War dominated politics. The Civil Rights Act of 1964 made it illegal to discriminate based on color, national origin, race, religion, and sex. Notable events included the assassinations Martin Luther King, Jr. and John F. Kennedy, the Cuban Missile Crisis, and the first man landing on the moon.

Fashion

The space age influenced people, and the "hippie" style emerged with psychedelic colors and patterns, and military influences. Afros, beehive, hippie hair, flipped bob, mop top, and Vidal Sassoon hair styles.

Technology

There were many inventions during the 1960s, including the cash dispenser, fiber optics, pacemakers, space travel, lasers, LEDs, the optical disk, the portable calculator, the cassette tape, and weather satellites.

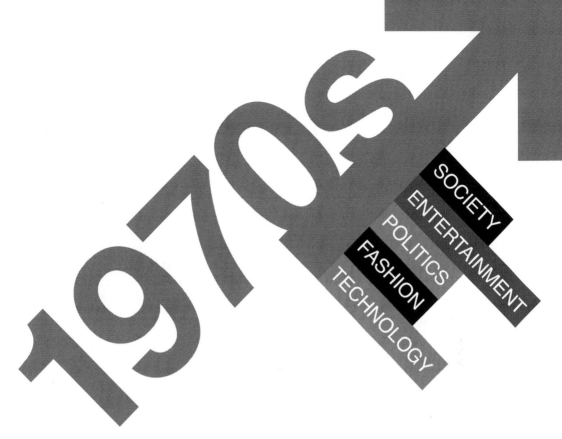

Society

Political and economic freedom for women, and gay rights, as well as increased crime and urban decay, economic struggle, cultural change, and technological innovation. Minimalism, conceptual art, and neo-expressionism became popular art movements.

Entertainment

Emergence of soap operas, jiggle television and crime shows, science fiction, daytime game shows, newscasts, telefilms, and variety shows. Horror movie classics like *The Exorcist*, and sci-fi cinema epics, such as *Star Wars*, crime epics, such as T*he Godfather*, psychological dramas, such as *One Flew Over the Cuckoo's Nest*, and musicals, like *Saturday Night Fever* were produced. Diverse and stylized music genres were also the norm: disco, funk, glam rock, heavy metal, krautrock, new wave, progressive rock, punk rock, soul, and synth-pop.

Politics

The rise of environmental movements, women's rights, and gay rights. The energy crisis, Watergate scandal, and the ongoing Vietnam War. The Iranian Revolution overthrew the Pahlavi dynasty with an Islamic republic. Margaret Thatcher became the first woman Prime Minister for the UK, as did Maria de Lourdes Pintasilgo for Portugal.

Fashion

Bell-bottom trousers, knee-high boots, platform shoes, flannel shirts, frayed jeans, midi skirts, ponchos, hot pants, chokers, headbands, feathers, and beads. Dreadlocks, feather cut, mohicans, perms, shag, wedge, long and straight hairstyles.

Technology

Invention of the barcode, e-mail, floppy disks, genetic engineering, ink-jet, laser printers, in-vitro fertilization, LCDs, microprocessors, MRI scanners, personal computers, and video games.

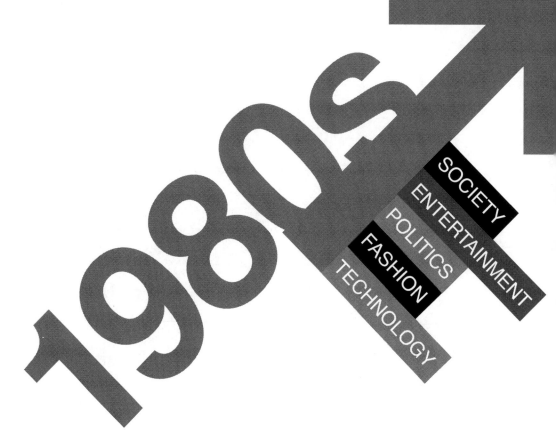

1980s

SOCIETY
ENTERTAINMENT
POLITICS
FASHION
TECHNOLOGY

Society
The Ethiopian famine, Exxon Valdez oil spill, Mount St. Helens' eruption, Chernobyl nuclear plant explosion, which resulted in a radioactive cloud that circled the world and caused thousands of deaths, and the bane of AIDS. John Lennon was assassinated. Microsoft created an operating system for IBM computers that forever changed the computing industry by making computers accessible and affordable to the masses. Graffiti art was popularized.

Entertainment
MTV transformed pop culture. Blockbuster movies, such as *ET: The Extra-Terrestrial* and *Raiders of the Lost Ark* engaged all ages, and a zenith period of teen movies, such as *The Breakfast Club* and *Pretty in Pink*. Artists like Public Enemy championed the voice of urban African Americans and cleared the way for hip hop. Acid house, break dancing, dance music, hair metal, house music, indie, new wave, rap, and synth-pop all emerged.

Politics
Conservative politics, "Reaganomics", and "Thatcherism" held sway. Race riots occurred in UK cities. The Falklands War between Argentina and the UK. The glasnost and perestroika

policies implemented by Soviet Premier Mikhail Gorbachev's marked the end of the Cold War. The collapse of the Berlin Wall to reintegrate East and West Germany.

Fashion
Ostentatious tastes, clothes, and fashion accessories mirrored wealth and power. Bold androgynous styles, colors, silhouettes, and excessive amounts of makeup. Leg warmers, power suits, puffed shoulders, and saturated colors. Crimps, curls, flattops, hi-top fades, mowaks, mullets, and perm hairstyles were all in style, marking one of the most eclectic decades in fashion for both sexes.

Technology
The advancement of answering machines, cable television, camcorders, CDs, cell phones, fax machines, Graphical User Interfaces (GUIs), personal computers, portable phones, VCRs, video game consoles, and Walkmans.

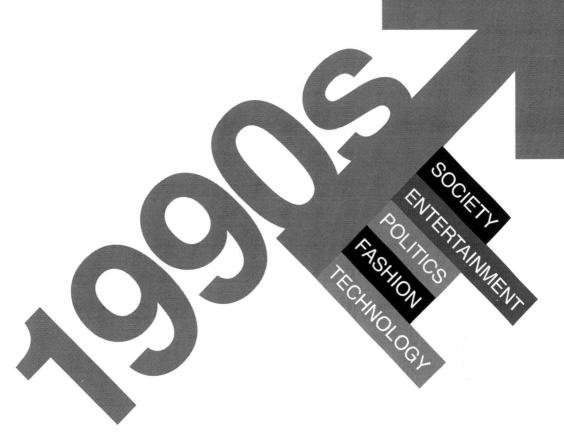

1990s

SOCIETY
ENTERTAINMENT
POLITICS
FASHION
TECHNOLOGY

Society

The Internet changed the world, how people communicated, and how business was done. The second half of the decade experienced strong economic growth with low unemployment, low inflation, improved productivity, and a strong stock market that resulted from a combination of rapid technological innovation and central monetary policy. Nelson Mandela was released after 27 years in captivity. "Grunge" was born as Seattle influenced how young people dressed and listened to music. Graffiti art, transgressive art, and activist art became popular forces throughout the decade.

Entertainment

Manufactured boy and girl-bands arose. Emergence of Britpop, grunge, industrial rock, and the fusion of multiple styles such as funk, jazz, and soul, which inspired g-funk, hip hop soul, new jack swing, and neo-soul genres. Some of the decade's most iconic movies include *Pulp Fiction, The Matrix, Jurassic Park, Blair Witch Project,* and *Toy Story.*

Politics

Major political events included the Gulf War, the triumph of capitalism after the collapse of the Soviet Union, the Warsaw Pact, the reunification of Germany, and the separation of Namibia from South Africa.

Fashion

The grunge subculture popularized colored plaid flannel shirts, ripped and stonewashed jeans, Birkenstocks, combat boots, Doc Martens, and high-top sneakers. Beach curls, blonde highlights, blunt cut, cornrows, curtains, feathered bangs, high braids, and pixie hairstyles.

Technology

The world wide web, mobile phones, text messages, DVDs, and gaming platforms like Nintendo all gained popularity.

2000s

SOCIETY
ENTERTAINMENT
POLITICS
FASHION
TECHNOLOGY

Society

The bursting of the dot-com bubble, Google's founding, social networking, the rise of YouTube, blogging, and podcasts. China became a superpower. Wars (Terrorism, Iraq) were fought, and the human genome was mapped. Hurricane Katrina caused deaths and billions in damage; earthquakes devastated Haiti, killing hundreds of thousands and destroying the country's infrastructure.

Entertainment

Video games became popular with the SEGA and the Nintendo release, and more advanced gaming consoles such as Xbox 360, PlayStation 2, and Game-Cube. Reality TV shows such as *American Idol, Big Brother,* and *Pop Idol,* also emerged. Innovations in Media distribution technology, digital TV technology and streaming, online video platforms, video-on-demand, and web TV occurred throughout the decade, accompanied by a significant increased content creation and television programs. Cloud rap, drill, emo, hip hop, and trap music became mainstream genres in popular music.

Politics

The 9/11 terrorist attacks befell New York City, Shanksville, Pennsylvania, and Washington DC. Al-Qaeda and affiliated Islamist militant groups executed terrorist acts throughout the decade, including the Bali bombings and the Istanbul bombings. A US-led coalition invaded Iraq as part of the War on Terror.

Fashion

Cargo pants, crop tops, hoodies, jean skirts, low-rise flared jeans, off the shoulder tops, platform sandals, ribbed sweaters, sneakers, and Ugg boots. Braided antennas, chunky highlights, curtain and side bangs, faux hawk, mermaid waves, softened swoop, spikey loop buns, and textured cut hairstyles.

Technology

The main technological advancements included the iPod, iPad, iPhone, and other smartphones, USB flash drives, Bluetooth, electric vehicles, Blu-ray discs, and social media, such as Facebook, YouTube, LinkedIn, and Twitter.

2010s

SOCIETY
ENTERTAINMENT
POLITICS
FASHION
TECHNOLOGY

Society

Natural disasters that had devasting effects included earthquakes and/or tsunamis in Haiti, Nepal, Sulawesi, Tōhoku, and numerous devastating hurricanes.

Entertainment

Game of Thrones dominated television, and the Marvel Cinematic Universe franchise subjugated the movie box offices. Amazon Music, Google Music, iTunes/Apple Music, and Spotify revolutionized how people consumed music by providing more convenient, accessible, and affordable solutions, which make it possible for consumers to listen to music from anywhere at any time.

Politics

The decade witnessed the presidencies of Barack Obama and Donald Trump. The US legalized same-sex marriage, as did other countries. marriage, as did other countries.

Fashion

Trends included a mix of hipster and athleisure fashion coupled with the revival of austerity-era period pieces, swag-inspired outfits, and unisex style elements. Beachy waves, lob cuts, man buns, messy buns, pompadour, side braids, tapered, and topknot hair styles.

Technology

Advancements included nanotechnology, electric vehicles, renewable energy, quantum computing, the Internet of Things, blockchain, machine learning, devices like the Kindle and iPad, virtual reality, and associated capabilities.

CONTEMPORARY
LIFE

COVID-19, a global pandemic, caused millions of deaths. It disrupted economies and societies globally, with millions of people falling into poverty. It affected people's lives and financial choices across every generation. It compelled society to reduce division, prioritize what matters the most, and come together to navigate the way forward universally.

STORYTELLERS
UNITE THE WORLD

Stories are the oxygen for communication. Storytelling is a language that unites the world. It brings us together, help us understand our past and reach toward the future. A well-told story engages the mind, heart, and soul.

As Maya Angelou poignantly drove home, "I've learned that people will forget what you said, people will forget what you did. But people will never forget how you made them feel." There is also an ancient proverb saying, "Tell me a fact, and I'll learn. Tell me the truth, and I'll believe, but tell me a story, and it will live in my heart forever."

Every culture has its own unique story to tell and narratives to educate, entertain, preserve, and guide moral values; they communicate joy, passions, fears, sadness, and hardships. Like music, stories are universal. They convey purpose and meaning and help us understand ourselves and find common ground with others.

Storytelling makes meaningful connections across history and time, uniting people by helping them make sense of themselves and the world. Insights are spread by passing knowledge from one generation to another, linking traditions, legends, myths, archetypes, culture, history, and values, which unite communities and societies.

David Llama, founder and Head of Creative at El Animal, has been on a lifelong quest to connect people via branded content and documentary filmmaking. His work is human-led and has a social purpose—making meaningful connections that help people make sense of themselves and the world they live in through art, design, products, advertising, digital publications, and print.

STORYTELLERS
UNITE THE
WORLD

"Growing up in Mexico City, surrounded by 24 million people, communicating with and socially interacting with people is a means of survival. If you do not know how to properly engage with people and tell a compelling story, you're limiting your opportunities to grow."

When the COVID-19 pandemic became global in March 2020, its mortality rate and economic and social impact were devasting. Social interaction was significantly curtailed. Governments had to mandate lockdowns restricting people to their homes to prevent gatherings. Virtual engagement replaced physical engagement as a means of connection.

David reacted to this by establishing a storytelling documentary series bringing together hundreds of people from across multiple countries to tell their stories. Stories about how the pandemic has affected their lives and relationships, their coping mechanisms, how they are entertaining themselves to keep spirits alive, and how they continue to be progressive in a temporary world where social gatherings and entertainment venues have shut down.

"I learned that, by bringing a diverse range of people across many countries together to share their insights and experiences, that we are more alike than different as humans, and that storytelling is the most powerful tool to share and understand our collective experiences, by providing comfort and hope," says David.

STORYTELLERS
UNITE THE
WORLD

Purposeful storytelling means being clear about your audience. What do they care about? What stories will resonate best with them? Why should they care? What is your goal? Is it to entertain? Is it to inspire? Is it to excite? Is it to influence? What's the call to action that you want your audience to take away? Most importantly how do you want to make them feel?

For as long as people have gathered together, we have been storytellers. The stories we tell make us human because we are fulfilled by creating and sharing something meaningful. Stories bring us together. They help us understand our past and reach toward the future. A well-told story engages the mind, heart, and soul. A powerful narrative is built from simple principles.

Truth is how we connect emotionally with a story and relate it to ourselves. By bringing genuine moments to life, and celebrating relationships between people rather than just facts about things, we can tell inspiring stories. We look for meaning in stories because we tell stories; they don't tell themselves.

Our chosen voice and style have the potential to reveal meaning with ease or bury it in confusion. The right style and voice will bring clarity to stories, both complex and straightforward, and what we say will be remembered.

STORYTELLERS UNITE THE WORLD

We exist in time. Our lives have beginnings, middles, and endings, filled with ups and downs, sudden reversals, and unexpected successes. Conflict is the engine of narrative; it's what keeps us listening. Details of the hope, frustration, and joy inherent in any journey deepen our narrative's impact.

We tell stories to share and understand human experiences - building connections and passing on wisdom. From the Mesopotamia to the Incas civilizations, the clans of the Hebrides to the Galápagos Islands, around campfires, in poetry, song, and throughout venues, stories celebrate our shared humanity.

4 CREATIVE SOCIETIES

CREATIVE
SOCIETIES

Understand how societies are a catalyst for inspiring creativity and sociocultural movements, where people can realize their full potential and live more enriched, fulfilled, and happy lives.

CREATIVE
SOCIETIES

Metropolises inspire creativity as a space for social integration, dreaming, making, and doing, where citizens can realize their full potential to live more enriched, fulfilled, and happy lives. Combined with the chemistry of individual human ingenuity, creative breakthroughs are a human process that happens when a diverse community of like-minded, purpose-led, and mission-driven creative people comes together.

Societies are a catalyst for creating influential art and sociocultural movements. This can be seen from the Ancient Egyptian Memphis, Classical Athens and Renaissance Florence to the French Revolution and Romanticism in Paris, to postwar New York and London. Historically, industrial cities like Detroit, Glasgow, and Manchester have an engrained maker and doer ethos, and port towns such as Amsterdam, Copenhagen, Dublin, and Liverpool have a constant exchange, diversity of people, and international trade. The modern-day digital revolution was born in Silicon Valley within the San Francisco Bay Area of California, with its burgeoning start-up and global technology innovation scene and its culture of openness and free exchange of ideas.

Creativity is a way of living. Creative hubs and the experiences gleaned through entrepreneurship and innovation improve people's lives, making societies more productive and improving the places where we live, work, and play. Setting the right conditions for the urban revolution is essential for a better life and society.

CREATIVE
SOCIETIES

Designing and operating a society is like a mixing desk that takes all the sources and attributes of society—cultural, economic, political, and technological—and, considering how to prioritize, combine, mix, and change the level and dynamics, brings them together into solutions that will deliver the outcome you want the society to be based on: the goals, principles, and policies you set, and how you operate and execute them.

The bottom line is that a creative society is where people are open-minded and have broad perspectives to overcome prejudices and obstacles. They feel empowered, free, and safe to express themselves and create without fear, and they approach problem solving openly and innovatively by trying out new ideas and ways of thinking and doing.

You cannot simply throw money at creative pursuits and expect instant results. It is a social system—made up of a network of relationships connected by a distinguishable similarity of spirit and shared values—which gravitates toward a coherent whole between individuals, groups, communities, cities, nations, corporations, and industries.

Societies like Dubai and Singapore are economically led with significant material investment injected into their societies combined with substantial wealth creation, which has led to high affluence. Conservative politics and strict laws tend to be unchallenged, where high police enforcement tends to drive a more rigid zero-tolerance approach and heightened censorship levels. While these societies have comparatively low crime, there is also a lack of diversity of thought, freedom of expression, and creativity.

CREATIVE
SOCIETIES

While the benefits of CCTV and constant surveillance can create a more safe and secure environment, it diminishes people's privacy and creates mistrust. While context, moderation, and balance are important, these factors ultimately tally up to being causes for their lack of creative output, especially in comparison to more liberated places like Amsterdam, Berlin, Copenhagen, Glasgow, London, Los Angeles, Manchester, New York City, and San Francisco. Yes, these cities all have their own unique quirks and flaws, though the common thread between them is that they put people and culture first, before economics. Therefore, they are not hampered, under compulsion or restraint. People there take ownership and feel safe being themselves.

A friend recently picked me up in his car near Lime Street Train Station in Liverpool. There was a queue within the car park, which delayed us from exiting by a few minutes, so we exceeded the 20-minute free parking curfew. As we approached the parking attendant to express our rational, he refused to cave in, and we had to pay. This sets the wrong tone and image for a city, making you less likely to return because it creates a negative impression that mushrooms. After all, you're going to share your experience with your friends and network, then that force multiplies.

Unfortunately, people with an axe to grind can sometimes gravitate toward these types of professions. For example, some of the North American border controls are particularly polarizing and pointlessly bureaucratic and obnoxious. They treat everyone with suspicion; a chancer or a prospective criminal, unlike cities like Johannesburg, where the airport customs officers are affable and pragmatic. Similarly, T5 at Heathrow is well designed to get you in and out of the terminal as quickly as possible.

CREATIVE
SOCIETIES

Despite its renowned solidity and organized society, Germany transformed itself multiple times throughout the 20th century; a monarchy, fascist dictatorship, communism, then democracy. Fear builds walls. The Berlin Wall separated East and West Germany from 1961 to 1989. Current day Berlin has become one of the most liberated and influential creative societies on the planet. A resilient and adaptive society, that's philosophical logic and reasoning to rationalize, combined with disciplined pragmatism, has made it a formidable force throughout time.

Asia is a mystic, erotic, and spiritually enlightening civilization. East Asia, specifically Japan, is particularly unique in its culture and traditions, partly because historically Japan has been isolated as a nation, which is reflected in many aspects of its culture. These characteristics have been developed without outside influence.

CREATIVE
SOCIETIES

The Japanese have a supernatural capability as systems thinkers, which is reflected in their precision in making products and offering services and experiences. Tokyo has been particularly influential in animation, arts, automotive, electronics, fashion, manufacturing, printing, publishing, and robots, and its transportation system is second to none. It is clean, reliable, punctual, and uncomplicated. Most people use the Shinkansen, trains, subways, and buses to commute to school and work.

Many artistic influences were diffused along the Silk Road, most notably the melding of Chinese, Buddhist, Greco, Hellenistic, Indian, and Iranian cultures. Here art was symbolic of religion and used as currency for trade across the network of land-based trade routes that connected the East and West from the 2nd to the 18th century.

Travel is a catalyst for inspiring innovation and creativity because you experience different cultures and diverse societies. Learning to appreciate and respect these differences in lifestyle and behavior unites us. Traveling forces us to depart from the familiar and take on a world of new experiences, cultures, languages, architectures, foods, and lifestyles, influencing our minds, bodies, and souls by shaping us into better, more well-rounded people with a more integrative worldview. We get exposed to and understand people's dynamics, life, cultures, subcultures, customs, religions, languages, governments, economies, and arts.

CREATIVE
SOCIETIES

Of course, idiosyncrasies exist, though fundamentally, people are the same everywhere in that we are all born, live, and die. Have loves, hates, and passions. The same core structure—brain, nerves, organs, and skin. We all need to breathe, drink, and eat to stay alive. What makes us unique is how we self-identify by discovering our own strengths and expressing our personalities, talents, and triumphs.

CREATIVE
SOCIETIES

Over half the world's population and three-quarters of its economic activity reside within cities. Urbanization is the nexus for culture and creativity and is the by-product of economic development because growth sectors of an economy are generally located in cities, where they benefit from an accumulation of economies, market access and concentrated skilled labor. Policies and solutions drive sustainable development and urban regeneration through cultural diversity, citizens' well-being, social cohesion, economic growth, and enriched and fulfilled lifestyles.

While cities like Athens, Buenos Aires, Cape Town, Chicago, Copenhagen, Dublin, Florence, Istanbul, Lisbon, Madrid, Melbourne, Mexico City, Montreal, Mumbai, Munich, Prague, Reykjavik, St. Petersburg, Stockholm, and Venice have made, and continue to make, their mark as creative cities, these sixteen cities have had a profound effect on the world's creative output over the last few centuries:

Creative societies

Creative hubs and the experiences gleaned through entrepreneurship and innovation improve people's lives, making societies more productive and improving the places where we live, work, and play.

AMSTERDAM

The city's trading roots, where productive collaborations were formed with many cultures to simplify trade and economic advancement, combines with a bohemian culture, which inspires creatives—most notably, Vincent van Gogh and Rembrandt van Rijn.

BARCELONA

A trend-setter in fashion, design, architecture, and music. Picasso, Gaudí, Miró, and Tàpies blessed this metropolis with iconic architecture and design.

BERLIN

Liberal policies and lower costs of living have formed the seedbed for its burgeoning avant-garde art, design, techno music, and fashion scenes.

DETROIT

Home of the innovator of the manufacturing assembly that brought the car revolution to the masses. Motown, one of the most influential record labels and music movements of all time. Numerous creatives born out of the city's engrained maker-and-doer ethos have graced the world with their art.

It has evolved from its industrial powerhouse roots into a creative and cultural center filled with artists, designers, creators, and innovators, who facilitate social integration.

GLASGOW

Its port town roots—infused with cultural wealth from Africa, the Americas, and Asia—influenced its artistic output; most famously The Beatles and Merseybeat in the 1960s, the Cavern Club (where many historical musical events were hosted), and Eric's Club, which hosted influential punk and post-punk bands of the 1970s and 1980s.

LIVERPOOL

A magnet for the creative industries, especially design, fashion, film, media, and music, as well as an influential technology industry. It was instrumental in developing punk music and new romantics, and it is the center for urban music, such as the UK garage, drum, bass, dubstep, and grime genres.

LONDON

The alleged "creative capital of the world" with a significant proportion of its inhabitants (actors, artists, dancers, filmmakers, musicians, and writers) living and working in the creative industry. Hollywood is revered as the destination for movie and television making.

LOS ANGELES

"The birthplace of the industrial revolution" and the main driving force behind the British indie music movement of the 1980s and the "Madchester" scene.

MANCHESTER

Renowned as the "fashion capital of the world" for its contribution to the fashion industry by setting the tone for and influencing global fashion trends and styles.

MILAN

The acclaimed "capital of the world" is a global powerhouse for its creative output in advertising, architecture, broadcasting, design, art, film, music, performing arts, publishing, television, and visual arts. The city provides unmatched exposure to cultural diversity, innovative ideas, and novel experiences, which inspire creativity and innovation globally.

NEW YORK CITY

The "city of art" synonymous with influential artists and art movements like; art deco, art nouveau, cubism, fauvism, impressionism, romanticism, and symbolism.

PARIS

ROME

The Vatican Museums alone earn Rome its place on any map of iconic art and architecture. The city's Cinecittà Studios play an institutional role in filmmaking, leaving a trail of influential legacy.

SAN FRANCISCO

The epicenter of American counterculture. The city's proximity to Silicon Valley has made it a world capital for the creative and technological invention and innovation that has revolutionized the post-industrial revolution.

TOKYO

An innovative powerhouse in anime culture, architecture, automobiles, consumer electronics, cyberpunk, design, fashion, food, gadgets, robotics, smartphones, and video games. While infused with eclectic American, Chinese, European, Greek, Indian, Jōmon, Korean, Greek, and Indian influences, its culture is distinctly unique, grounded in continuous learning and improvement.

VIENNA

Synonymous with classical music and birthplace to many revered composers like Schubert, Strauss (I and II) and Maria Theresia von Paradis. Others such as Beethoven, Berg, Haydn, Klimt, Mozart, Clara Schumann, flocked there to establish themselves in the musical scene.

TIME, PLACE, OCCASION

Creativity inspires urban development, which lures bohemians and artists with the attraction of being exposed to innovative ideas and like-minded people. Innovations are more likely to happen in urban areas than in rural areas, drawing more creatives to these open-minded, modern, and progressive communities and the culture and amenities that come with them.

Conditions need to be established for people to dream, make, and do as a collective ecosystem. Architecture, the environment, incentives, and regulatory regimes must be developed to realize this. A skilled and dynamic workforce made up of dreamers, makers, and doers forms a social system with distinct values, attitudes, and feelings learned and transmitted from each generation.

In ancient Greek mythology, creativity was believed to have been handed down from the gods—specifically the Muses, who gave artists and philosophers the necessary inspiration for creation. Humans who were creators were closer in connection to these divine sources. This dovetailed and evolved into many aspects of Greek and later Roman society, specifically in law, policy making, democratic government practices, language, literature, art, infrastructure, and city planning.

Until the industrial revolution in the 18th century, the majority of people lived on farms, living off the land and human-made economic production in rural societies with no mass production or provision to transport large quantities of goods over long distances. Structured education was a rarity. Disease and malnutrition were rife. Homegrown products and services were produced and traded within their immediate community. The quickest form of transportation was the speed of a horse, and businesses were cottage industries, where people or animals produced a limited amount of goods.

TIME, PLACE, OCCASION

The industrial revolution blew this model wide open through technological innovation that changed how people lived and how work got done. Tasks that had once taken months were reduced to taking days. Machines replaced manual labor. Education and health care radically improved. Urban centers were created as magnets for factory production and employment. People flocked from all over to live and work in cities. The downside of this rapid growth in urbanization was that cities did not have sufficient infrastructure and provision to accommodate this population influx, leading to overcrowding, congestion, poverty, and crime.

The Gorbals personified this darker side of the industrial revolution, hunched like a Gothic recidivist imposing dismay on Glasgow's heaving slums. The Gorbals was densely populated, largely with immigrants, attracted to the city to rebuild their lives. They sought jobs in new industries and lived in cramped, unsanitary, poverty-stricken, criminally vulgar tenements. Rage was further fueled by sectarianism in religious and political rivalry between Roman Catholics and Protestants.

TIME, PLACE, OCCASION

The resilient Glasgow, once an industrial powerhouse, turned into a post-modern creative magnet. It gained a reputation as the second city, after London, of the British Empire throughout much of the Victorian, Edwardian, and Georgian periods through its marine engineering, shipbuilding, and manufacturing prowess. Its architectural prowess is its homegrown 'Glasgow Style' Mackintosh architecture, a blend of Celtic and Japanese art, inspired by Wiener Werkstätte, Bauhaus, Vienna Secession, and Deutscher Werkbund. The city has a clan-like culture, and its community lacks hierarchy. It is people-focused and action-oriented, and one's patter is mightier than one's sword. It's comedic, idiosyncratic, and off-the-cuff observational wit (personified by Billy Connolly) and its burgeoning music scene (most notably featuring Alan Horne and Edwyn Collins' sophistipop label Postcard Records, which brought Orange Juice, Joseph K, and Aztec Camera to the world) influenced many independent musicians and pop movements throughout the 1980s. Glasgow's answer to popular culture, Svengali Malcolm McLaren and Alan McGee, established Creation Records as a major force in 1980s and 1990s independent music and popular culture, most notably with The Jesus and Mary Chain and Primal Scream. Glasgow's most famous musical sons, Simple Minds, created their own ark in the late 1970s and have sailed it across the music ether ever since to universal appeal and glory by producing staples such as *Real to Real Cacophony, Chelsea Girl,* and *I Travel*, and their seminal *New Gold Dream* album.

TIME, PLACE, OCCASION

""Brave and noble" Manchester was the birthplace of the industrial revolution. It was built on new ideas and inventions within a thriving industrialized maker-and-doer urbanized society. Red brick warehouses, railway viaducts, textile mills, and canals are remnants of its industrial past, combined with a diverse mixture of art deco, art nouveau, brutalist, Edwardian, Georgian, medieval, modernist, neo-classical, neo-Gothic, palazzo, Venetian Gothic, and Victorian architectural styles. Its transportation infrastructure, such as its canals and railway system, provided links to the world. Unlike other cities such as Seattle, San Francisco, and Chicago, which have experienced snapshots in time for their musical and pop culture influence, Manchester has engineered a prolonged and self-sustaining musical output that has navigated time with a no-nonsense attitude and confident swagger—Buzzcocks, Magazine, Joy Division, New Order, The Smiths, James, Happy Mondays, The Stone Roses, Inspiral Carpets, and Oasis. Cultural catalyst Tony Wilson championed local bands. His record label, Factory Records, which he co-founded with Alan Erasmas, Rob Gretton, and Martin Hannett, put them out to the wider world coupled with The Haçienda nightclub, which enabled a whole new scene in dance music.

TIME, PLACE,
OCCASION

The post-industrial revolution led to the creation of digital societies in Europe, Japan, and the U.S.A, which led to the services industry producing more wealth than traditional industries based on the information and services produced by technology titans like Apple, Google, IBM, Microsoft, and Oracle. The largest and most influential hub of technology-enabled creativity and innovation is Silicon Valley, in the San Francisco Bay Area of California, renowned for its innovative mindset, entrepreneurial spirit, and technology-based wealth creation. As with the industrial revolution, the digital revolution's impact has provided a new set of tools, aesthetics, and values.

ARCHITECTURE AND DESIGN
CHANGES HOW PEOPLE FEEL

Architecture and design influence how people feel and connect them emotionally. They speak a global language that everyone can understand regardless of their native language and cultural identity. They can affect how art is made and experienced, and they act as a catalyst for social integration and collaboration, empowering people with a sense of escapism, freedom, and hope to become self-actualized and live a fulfilled life.

Music venues like the Cavern Club in Liverpool became an epicenter for Merseybeat in the 1960s. The Troubadour in Los Angeles for folk music in the 1960s and 1970s. CBGB in New York City and the 100 Club in London for punk in the 1970s. The Wigan Casino for northern soul in the 1970s. In Manchester, the Haçienda nightclub for acid house, rave music, and the "Madchester" scene in the late 1980s and early 1990s. These venues became synonymous with the music they hosted. A sanctuary where music, fashion, and culture came together where like-minded people could self-identify and feel liberated.

Modernist architecture pioneer Le Corbusier reinvented industrial housing into tenement buildings that mirrored streets at ground level and maximized space. Stanley Kubrick used these principles in his movie *A Clockwork Orange* to create a futuristic world. As did the designers of Park Hill, a public housing estate in Sheffield, England, inspired by Le Corbusier's *"Streets in the Sky"*; the spirit this place evoked was captured sonically within some of the early recordings of the city's local synth-pop band The Human League. Similarly with Hulme Crescents in Manchester and Quarry Hill Estate in Leeds.

"While growing up in Sheffield, you would constantly hear the industrious sound of machinery, which was as commonplace as birds on the trees if you lived in the countryside. This was subconsciously infused within the music we made." said Martyn

ARCHITECTURE AND DESIGN CHANGES HOW PEOPLE FEEL

Ware, founder of The Human League, Heaven 17, record producer, entrepreneur, educator, and activist.

Brutalism followed the modernist blueprint, where form followed function to design buildings that resembled what they are, such as the Barbican in London—one of the finest manifestations of the Brutalist utopian style for inner-city living. Another architectural and design marvel of industrial Britain was the magnificent art deco style Battersea Power Station, which dominated the London skyline for generations and was an endless source of inspiration for many music videos, films, and television programs.

Frank Lloyd Wright built an architecture that represented the vast American landscape's unique identity, its diversity of people, and its democratic ideals of freedom through his organic architectural design. Form followed function where the building, furnishings, environment, and surroundings became part of a unified and interrelated composition. This was most famously manifested in Fallingwater, a design from which its inhabitants could see, hear, and feel nature.

The art nouveau and art deco style Glaswegian architect Charles Rennie Mackintosh put Scotland on the architectural map as a center for creativity with his re-design of the Glasgow School of Art that infused symbolist architectural style, rigorously designed to the last detail, with Japonism minimalism, and floral motifs. Another architectural staple is the cantilever trussed Forth Bridge that crosses Scotland's Firth of Forth estuary.

UTOPIAN FUTURES: A WORLD REBOOTED

Imagine if the world was rebooted to its factory settings. Not a hard reboot, where everything was erased, but one that would reset our way of living, allowing us to return to the previous setting and ignore the changes made in recent years.

What would you do differently if there were no constraints?

Imagine a value system that rewarded people for their contribution to others, and that didn't oppose success. Instead, it would encourage a person to strive not just for excellence and artistry, but would reward hard work in math, science, and engineering with the same merit as sculpture, dance, or art. It would level the playing field with opportunities for every single person to embrace what they love to do by enabling and encouraging people to follow their passions as a career rather than tolerating jobs they loathed. It would recognize that the environment is for everyone to enjoy, not pillage. It would embed sustainability and the principles of the circular economy as unimpeachable pillars of humanity, and it would encourage sharing to reduce conflict. It would allow us to embrace choice, but never at the expense of others. Finally, it would reward hard work and require continued contributions from each generation.

Utopian? Of course! By definition, it has to be; after all, it is a future designed to be better, not worse. Starting with a utopian vision is important because it enables us to break free of today's problems by seeing the potential of what could be. Where do we start? Start with what matters most by defining and prioritizing a set of core principles that your utopia is founded upon. The prioritization is essential because when conflicting objectives arise, the ranking simplifies the choice.

UTOPIAN FUTURES: A WORLD REBOOTED

Take a people-first approach

Start by putting people first. They are the heart of the system. This means putting people's happiness, health, and wealth at the center of all things. Policy and regulation are grounded in transparency, honesty, and trust that flows into the value system of people's everyday behavior, ensuring safety, well-being, and happiness. Every other principle segues from this throughout an interconnected societal nervous system.

Live sustainably

Life is dependent on healthy living and environment for the likes of food, air, water, and clean ecosystems that purify the air, maintain soil, regulate climate, recycle nutrients, and provide food. Failing to live sustainably increases costs not only in cleaning the environment to free it from pollution and damage but also in increased healthcare and social costs.

Level the playing field by raising it for everyone

Install the infrastructure, systems, and ecosystems across all aspects of society to reward contribution to society. Define success by what individuals contribute to society based on their individual talents, abilities, and effort instead of valuing their salary and the assets of family connections and entitlement.

This means ignoring political labels like communism, socialism, and capitalism, and government forms such as monarchy, oligarchy, democracy, republic, and anarchy. Rise above these by focusing on human values. Define a society based on fairness and equality. This does not mean everybody earning the same amount. If you work hard, you can realize the benefits of this.

UTOPIAN FUTURES:
A WORLD REBOOTED

A "level playing field" means a society open to everyone. This is often misrepresented as having equal opportunities, employment, and diversity monitoring. However, it is far more fundamental than this. It means a commitment from the very start of life to providing an environment that allows everyone to live a self-determined life, in which they are free to explore the opportunities created by and open to them. It means ensuring that we provide opportunities to all, regardless of their family income or wealth.

It doesn't start with education or equality of employment. It starts before this. A level playing field means having secure and safe housing, having quality schooling at all levels, and being able to follow your passion without having to worry about being burdened with debt while you learn. It means having access to healthcare without having to worry about the cost of treatment, and having the option to look after children or return to work.

UTOPIAN FUTURES: A WORLD REBOOTED

Embrace diversity and difference

Embracing diversity helps us both understand each other and ourselves. Recognizing and respecting our individual differences in gender, sexual orientation, race, ethnicity, age, physical abilities, social and economic status, religious and political beliefs, and other ideologies needs to be the norm, accepted without question. When people feel included, they build meaningful social relationships, have a stronger sense of belonging, and inspire creativity and innovation in themselves and others. The purpose of societal development is to provide leading-edge thinking, practice, and programs. Creating and curating a culture of thinking, learning, and doing is how people learn and pass on information. The more you interact and collaborate with people from different cultural backgrounds, disciplines, industries, and geographies the more you understand, respect, and value them, and the more enriched and fulfilled your life experience will be. We all benefit from learning from others.

Simplicity means the greatest levels of acceptance and engagement.

Policies need to remove complexity and be defined to provide clarity without requiring interpretation, to be well-thought through, widely shared, and designed to be meaningful for people. They should be prioritized for people over corporations, with clearly defined rights to encourage active participation in a fair society. Life should be lived without pollution or fear. We should have access to housing, education, and healthcare, and ultimately control our own bodies and destiny.

UTOPIAN FUTURES: A WORLD REBOOTED

Education Reversed

Education is the key to success, yet we do not educate how we learn. We live in the 21st century, but our education systems were designed to meet the bygone needs of the Victorian industrial age, where recall was valued over imagination. We have an education system that benevolently steers children away from the subjects they like, instead mandating a teaching model based on ease of administration and replicability. Early specialization, teaching to test, and micromanagement, instead of embracing creativity and flexible unstructured learning, deliver us a model that destroys free thought and crushes innovation.

Diversity and choice are marginalized in a one size fits all system. The new order is a modern education system that instills creativity as a core discipline at the grassroots and is nurtured throughout the educational system (which recognizes intelligence as multi-faceted); it embraces emotional and social intelligence, critical thinking, and practical problem solving and integrates science, arts, and humanities as equal parts of the learning jigsaw. The goal is to instill creative confidence through blended learning programs. It is also to encourage learning that zig-zags across disciplines and domains with continuous learning pathways that are open to anyone willing to invest effort and time to advance their knowledge, values, and skills. It is important to building a set of beliefs and moral habits to prepare and qualify people for work and social integration with a shared purpose and collaborative culture. The result is better health and well-being, increased social trust, greater political interest, reduced cynicism, greater engagement, and a population that embraces diversity and difference.

UTOPIAN FUTURES:
A WORLD REBOOTED

Leaders without frontiers

Society needs authentic leadership with the vision and know-how to make things happen by pushing humanity forward and making society better. Our chosen political leaders need to constantly challenge the status quo and stand against oppressive forces that diminish or oppose society, articulating their opinions and ideas without fear of retaliation. Leaders fearless in their expression should use their visions to fuel consistent action to bring to life ideas that push humanity forward.

We need to attract, select, and retain leaders who are empathetic, who deeply understand, and who are devoted to advancing people and society's needs. They should exercise their influence and power to make and enforce laws for society to function in the right way, predictably and safely. Providing the best conditions for humanity by setting and managing the right conditions; culturally, economically, politically, and technologically by enabling society to achieve self-actualization.

Mahatma Gandhi and Martin Luther King, Jr. led with a nonviolent approach, influencing later resistance by global movements. Nelson Mandela rebelled against the apartheid regime aiming to remove racism and eradicate poverty and inequality in South Africa. He defied all odds to become President. Abraham Lincoln enacted measures to oppose and abolish slavery in the U.S.A. Winston Churchill inspired people, had unique strategic insight, and refused to give in to evil during extreme adversity; he led the way to protect Great Britain and the Commonwealth's freedom by rallying a nation and forming strategic alliances with the USA and the Soviet Union in defiance of Hitler and the Nazi regime.

UTOPIAN FUTURES:
A WORLD REBOOTED

These leaders stood for purpose, reason, and conviction by seeing their policies through to the bitter end with resilience, grit, and the solitary intent of making humanity better. They did things that had never been done before. They rejected failure and swam against the tide to provide novel solutions to complex problems that we didn't know could exist, forming a new movement, culture, and new norms and ways of life.

These leaders were flawed and made mistakes, though as they matured, learned, and reflected, they were all ultimately driven by one common characteristic—they wanted a better world, and a better outcome for humanity!

Make politics attractive for authentic leaders.
Would you board a plane if the pilot did not know how to fly it? Would you allow your child to go to school if the teacher could not teach? Would you trust a doctor incapable of treating medical conditions? No! Why elect people who are not skilled and experienced as politicians who end up at the helm in influential positions that ultimately affect people's well-being and society. Or worse, privileged and entitled narcissists whose misguided motives and prejudices are kryptonite to the free world, which has been the case in some countries throughout time.

Authentic leaders are not compelled to politics in modern times. They tend to gravitate towards the humanities, arts, technology, entrepreneurship, and business. There may be monetary reasons for this, though a fundamental issue is their lack of trust and exhaustion of the old economy and its decayed political systems, coupled with the ethics and incompetence of people leading countries who do not have the empathy, skills, and experience to lead. It's time to reinvent politics and the types of leaders that need to be at the helm of society.

UTOPIAN FUTURES: A WORLD REBOOTED

Creativity exists within every single person, not the elite few.
Creativity is ordinary people doing extraordinary things. Creativity can be applied to every profession and domain because it is found in all aspects of life. It isn't something lost with age, but rather a skill we too often neglect to practice. The challenge is not learning new things, as this will inevitably happen as we explore, travel, learn, and grow. Rather, the challenge is keeping our childlike wonder and imagination alive and having the courage to combine those things with our new experiences and insight.

Flush the stereotypes and lead without frontiers.
Free your perception that you need the prerequisites to be in the creative arts and paint masterpieces like Dalí and Picasso did. Reject convention by identifying new and better ways of doing things with your eyes wide open and not by making ego-driven decisions; stay competitive, constantly hunt for new and better ways of doing business, eradicate excess, reduce waste, and benefit society. Recognize the allure and danger of the status quo. We are programmed to welcome stability and have an aversion to change, but this is the trap that prevents progress because all forms of growth require change.

Forbid the cynicism of failure: Win or learn mentality.
Foster a win or learn mentality. Allowing personal failure to trump you is kryptonite to the soul and will crush your energy, imagination, and, ultimately, your creativity. Embrace lifelong emotional and social learning where everything is possible. Passion is energy. Be connected to something greater, be present, be accountable and excuse-free, and live to give.

UTOPIAN FUTURES:
A WORLD REBOOTED

Empower people to adapt as fast as society needs.
To nurture a culture of agility means being adaptive to constant change, fast-thinking, quick decision-making, driving autonomy, and empowering people to act quickly by smashing through obstacles to innovate and make progress. It means being liberal, inclusive, and meritocratic, yet remaining entirely focused and motivated to expedite the mission at hand. When we do this, we eradicate destructive blocks to a better society.

Don't get mesmerized by technology and being fooled into believing that it is the answer.
Ilt is not. As former Pixar Chief Creative Officer John Lassiter accurately declared: "Computers don't create computer animation any more than pencils create pencil animation. What creates is the artist." The key is the intelligent application of technology to unlocking human ingenuity for the greater good by pushing society forward ethically and responsibly. Humans and machines are working together to problem-solve and transform the world for the better in an "age of creativity".

The children of this revolution are the canvas onto which our values will be imprinted and shaped. Seamlessly woven into this is the responsibility to pass the baton by leaving the world better than we inherited it. Our next generation needs to be nurtured by parents committed to not repeating previous generations' mistakes. It is important to be socially conscious, self-confident, achievement-oriented, ambitious, technologically sophisticated, inquisitive, and driven to demand that those with authority accept responsibility and accountability. Above all, future generations should question explanations like "because this is the way it has always been done" and ask, "but is this the best way it can be done?" Start with youth to build the society of the future by taking a long-term approach.

CHAOS
TO
CULTURE

CHAOS
TO
CULTURE

How to nurture a culture of creativity through a do-it-yourself sensibility and a social system that allows people to create without fear and which is embraced, nurtured, imparted, and practiced by individuals, teams, and organizations; backed up with proven examples from creative industry experts.

Chaos to Culture

EMPOWERMENT THROUGH SHARED VISION, VALUES AND PRINCIPLES

DREAM I MAKE I DO

↓

**PURPOSE LED
MISSION-DRIVEN**

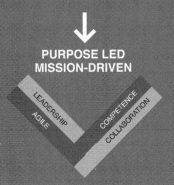

LEADERSHIP
AGILE
COMPETENCE
COLLABORATION

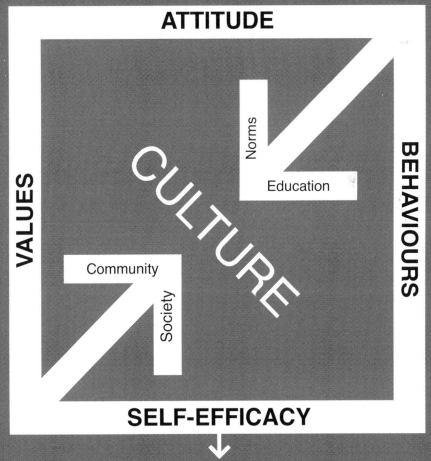

ATTITUDE

VALUES

BEHAVIOURS

CULTURE

Norms

Education

Community

Society

SELF-EFFICACY

↓

DISCOVERY I INVENTION I INNOVATION I CREATION

SEDITIOUS
EPIGRAMS

Art is culture, and culture is everywhere, connecting to our imagination, which might otherwise be untapped. Cultures are defined by the people who live and function within them. In the same demographic, two cultures created simultaneously, pursuing the same ideals, will still become two very different entities. Why? Because people are different. When people come together in the service of something greater, they retain their own unique personalities, passions, hopes, and dreams. The shared experiences and constant interactions between people make up a culture. Culture is the engine that drives our momentum. It is the sum of what you feel, believe, and do that shapes and defines your work's input and output.

The principles for curating creative cultures are:

Principles

1 LEADERSHIP

Leading by action to find the future by breaking through the status quo is leadership. Leaders create clarity by synthesizing complex concepts. They generate energy by inspiring optimism, creativity, and growth, and they deliver success by driving innovation and tenaciously pursuing the right outcomes.

2 DO-IT-YOURSELF

This means rejecting conventions and originating new ideals. Do-it-yourself refers to the rebellious impetuosity of non-conformity with direct action and not selling out; doing it in your own style and pace. Embrace challenge, accept failure, persist in the face of setbacks, and learn by doing as the path to mastery.

3 CRAFTSMANSHIP

Being passionately dedicated to your craft evokes wonder and discovery. Remaining honest, trustworthy, and responsible by taking pride in everything you do helps you achieve the highest quality craft and professional excellence levels.

4 COLLABORATION

It is important to collaborate when exploring new ideas, finding innovative solutions, and not being afraid to learn. Collaboration is the cross-pollination and sharing of knowledge across multiple domains by combining individuals' intellectual capital and know-how.

5 MENTORSHIP

Stand on the shoulders of giants by seeking counsel from people you trust, respect, and admire. Find positive role models who can share their skills, insights, and expertise to help nurture your ideas. Understand and respect history, and infuse best practices into finding the future to truly innovate and not reinvent the wheel.

culture

Social cultural movements

A social and cultural movement encompasses ideals, sensibilities, art, and science and is usually a reaction against prior movements and the status quo, which has grown uniform and monotonous. They can influence art, fashion, music, and popular culture and drive progressive change in politics and society, just as these British and American subcultures have over the last 70 years.

ACID HOUSE

Emerged as a subgenre of house music in the mid-1980s by DJs in Chicago. It is defined by "squelching" sounds and deep basslines of electronic bass synthesizer-sequencers.

BEATNIKS

Born of the 1950s literary, they rejected materialism, experimented with drugs and spiritual and sexual liberation. They listened to jazz music, and wore sandals, black turtlenecks, black berets, and goatee beards.

BLACK POWER

Influenced by the 1960s civil rights movement, pan-Africanism, black nationalist and socialist ideologies. They fashioned black styles, like full afros, and embraced soul music.

BOHEMIANS

Most prominent throughout the 1960s. Antiestablishment political and social viewpoints manifested through their alternative lifestyle, free love, frugality, and voluntary poverty.

Fought and intimidated supporters of rival soccer teams, most prominently throughout the 1980s. They fashioned Italian brands and ostentatious sportswear like Ellesse, Fila, and Tacchini. Caesar cuts, mod haircuts, shaved heads, and they listened to acid house, indie, "Madchester," and new wave music.

CASUALS

Founded in 2018 as a global environmental movement, Extinction Rebellion campaigns governments to address climate change and biodiversity loss and mitigate the risk of ecological and social demise. The "Red Rebels" dress in red to signify the blood of species that have lost their lives due to climate change's detrimental impact. .

EXTINCTION REBELLION

The glam rock movement in the 1970s was a reaction to the rock mainstream, manifested through heavy guitar and stomping rhythmic sonic, androgynist imagery, futuristic clothes and makeup, glittery boots, and striped patterns.

GLAM ROCKERS

Emerged in the 1980s from post-punk, marked by its emphasis on anti-conservative politics, individuality, and sexual diversity. Backcombed hairstyles, and dark Gothic styles like fishnet hosiery and skirts, leggings, combat boots, Doc Martens, pale flesh tone foundation and darkly colored eye makeup, manifested in bands like Bauhaus, The Cure, Siouxsie and the Banshees.

GOTHS

Associated with 1950s rock 'n' roll culture, rebels who rejected the mainstream attitudes and beliefs of the time manifested in Marlon Brando, James Dean, and Elvis Presley. Fashioned long greased hair, blue jeans, T-shirts, leather jackets, striped, checkered, and madras shirts, sneakers, and boots.

GREASERS

This electronic music genre ascended in the early 2000s in London that drew influences from dancehall, hip hop, and jungle. Its style included tracksuits and branded sportswear like Adidas, Nike, and Puma.

GRIME

Originated in Seattle in the early 1990s, as a subgenre of alternative rock inspired by hard-core punk, heavy metal, and alternative rock. Personified by angst-fueled lyrics, growling vocals, and distorted guitars. Layered clothing, such as a flannel shirts over a band T-shirt.

GRUNGE

This genre was born in the 1970s, popularizing leather battle jackets, combat boots, black jeans, camouflage trousers and shorts, studded belts, iron crosses, war souvenirs, badges, pins and patches. Styles included machoistic beards, moustaches and shoulder length hair, and woman heavily dyed back combed hair.

HEAVY METAL

HIP HOPPERS

Emerged in the 1980s, the social sentiment represented the marginalized youth, personified by the creative Black and Latino communities through MCing, DJing, b-boying, and graffiti art

HIPPIES

This 1960s subculture embraced the sexual revolution and "flower power" passive resistance and nonviolent opposition to the Vietnam War. Affiliated to protest folk musicians and psychedelic music. Styled in long hair, beads, blue bell-bottom jeans, ethnic clothing, headbands, floppy hats, flowing scarves, flower power motifs, peace symbols, and tie-dyed T-shirts.

HIPSTERS

Surfaced in the early 2000s as independent thinkers with progressive political views and a penchant for art and indie rock, styled in pompadour haircuts, beards, vintage attire, checked shirts, and skinny jeans.

MADCHESTER

Cultivated in Manchester in the late 1980s, it infused alternative rock, indie music, 1960s pop and psychedelic music, with acid house and rave music. Styled in bowl cuts and center partings, flared jeans, and baggy streetwear. Factory Records and its nightclub, The Haçienda, were pivotal in the development of the scene.

MODS

This 1960s subculture stood for modernist beliefs in fashion, music, and social status. Mods wore tailor-made suits, bowling shoes, brogues, desert boots, loafers, parkers, slim-fitting trousers, miniskirts, geometrical patterns on brightly colored clothes. Caesar, French crop and layered cuts were the popular hairstyles. They listened to soul, rhythm and blues, ska, jazz, and freakbeat and drove Lambretta and Vespa scooters.

NEW ROMANTICS

The Blitz club in London, ran by Steve Strange, was influential in launching this subcultural movement. Influenced by Marc Bolan, David Bowie, and Roxy Music, glam rock and the early Romantic period of the previous two centuries.

NEW WAVE

The new wave was born out of the punk movement at the beginning of the 1980s, personified by more accessible and commercially viable electronic music and a distinct visual style displayed in music videos and fashion, inspired by 1960s pop music and 1950s fashion.

NORTHERN SOUL

Emerged in the 1970s from the British mod scene in the midlands and north of England, inspired by Motown and American soul music. Men wore baggy trousers, brogues, knitted tanks, vests, and Fred Perrys, while women wore patterned slim fit shirts, and ankle-length circle skirts. Up-tempo dancing involved backdrops, flips, spins, and Bruce Lee influenced karate kicks.

Emerged in New York and London in the 1970s with antiestablishment and left-wing political views, promoting individual freedom and do-it-yourself ethics, centered on loud, aggressive rock music. They wore bondage trousers, chains, denim, kutte vests, leather, metal spikes and studs, military-style boots, and torn clothing. Haircuts included spiked hair, native American-inspired Mohican and Mohawk styles.

PUNK

Rappers attained popularity in the 1980s and 1990s through their rhythmic and rhyming speech music. Stylized in basketball jerseys, large hoodies in bright colors, baggy polo shirts, button-downs, and loose T-shirts with graphic prints.

RAP

Rave culture emerged in the late 1980s by using unauthorized abandoned spaces, such as industrial warehouses, to conduct raves for people to dance to fast-paced percussive electronic dance music, typically under the influence of drugs. Dressed in crop tops, glow in the dark clothing, overalls, phat pants, skin-tight outfits, smiley faces, and visors.

RAVERS

Surfaced in the 1960s Jamaican street culture associated with ska, punk, rocksteady, and 2 tone music. Rude Boys were into basketweave shoes, braces, Doc Martens, Harrington jackets, mohair, tonic and houndstooth suits, polo shirts, pork pie hats, and sta-prest trousers.

RUDE BOYS

Originated in the late 1950s and became prominent in the 1980s with an independent and free-thinking spirit, using skateboards to express themselves through freestyling and trickery. Stylized in baggy sportswear, baseball caps, basketball shoes, plaid shirts, and sleeveless T-shirts.

SKATERS

Formed among working-class youths in 1960s London. Styled in aggressively masculine hair and dress styles; shaved heads, bomber jackets, and heavy boots. Influenced by glam rock bands, punk rock, reggae, rocksteady, and 2 tone music genres.

SKIN HEADS

Born in southern California in the 1960s, this hedonistic subculture spread worldwide by surf-film cinematographers, surf magazines, and artists such as The Beach Boys, Jan and Dean, and The Surfers. Inspiring dance crazes such as The Frog, The Stomp, and The Watusi.

SURFERS

This subgenre of new wave music emerged in the late 1970s and featured drum machines, sequencers, and synthesizers. Pioneered by Kraftwerk, it was brought to mainstream pop music in the early to mid-1980s. Popularized by Depeche Mode, Gary Numan, Human League, Japan, and Orchestral Maneuvers in the Dark.

SYNTH POP

SOCIAL SYSTEMS THAT MAKE HISTORY

Creativity can't be subscribed to or bought off the shelf. It's a social system that encompasses values, skills, craftsmanship, relationships, networks, and a way of living and doing. It isn't simply a mandate that gets handed down. Creativity needs to be embraced to allow people to create without fear. It's something that is nurtured, imparted, and practiced throughout a team or an organization. It takes skill, practice, and persistence, but the results pay off, influencing society by changing opinions, instilling values, and translating experiences.

Culture catalysts make the invisible visible. They work behind the scenes to curate and influence a movement by assembling, cataloging, managing, and presenting the artistic and cultural importance of media, publications, and other expression venues. Fearless, charismatic, and bold risk takers see around the corner, embrace and expose unusual and unexpected themes and sources, and make bold statements about their passions and beliefs. Berry Gordy did precisely this for Motown. Brian Epstein did it with The Beatles, Andrew Oldham with The Rolling Stones, Andy Warhol with The Velvet Underground, Malcolm McLaren with the Sex Pistols, and Tony Wilson with Factory Records. These mavericks' passion for their craft paid off because they never feared to provoke action that changed minds and created a cultural movement.

Music is the language of the world with no boundaries. It unites and brings people together regardless of time and space, and it can change the world, affect a mood, atmosphere, and behavior, and captures a moment in time. Motown is a crowning poster child of this.

SOCIAL SYSTEMS THAT MAKE HISTORY

The Motown sound's charming and distinctive melodies, fronted by call-and-response singing, remained true to the "KISS" (keep it simple, stupid) principle by avoiding complex arrangements and elaborate and evocative vocal riffs. It also used a factory production system, inspired by founder and owner Berry Gordy's stint working at Ford's assembly line. He observed fabrication, assembly, and how products constructed from raw materials were brought to market globally. Gordy translated this into the music-making and artist-grooming process and invented a repeatable hitmaking machine with global resonance and appeal.

The Bauhaus movement's primary artistic ideology was to use art synergistically to revolutionize Germany's architecture through creativity and modernity based on a minimalist approach with clean lines and shapes, smooth, gentle curves, and bold, simple coloration. Bauhaus stood for the anxieties about modern manufacturing's soullessness and the fear that art was losing social relevance.

The New York City subway system signage was a hodge-podge of lettering sizes, materials, colors, styles, and messages. Creating a chaotic experience for commuters until Helvetica typography was introduced in the 1980s as the standard signage and became ubiquitous. Resulting in bringing structure to chaos and improving how commuters navigate their journeys.

SOCIAL SYSTEMS THAT MAKE HISTORY

The Specials fashioned a mod-style Rude Boy look with pork pie hats, tonic and mohair suits, and loafers. Anti-racism was intrinsic to their manifesto, integrating black and white performers and drawing on musical influences and styles largely influenced by Afro-Caribbean ska. Their aesthetic and sound were political and captured the disaffection and anger felt by the UK's youth due to dire economic and political conditions in Thatcherite Britain. They acted as a signpost for change to address the urban decay, deindustrialization, unemployment, and violence in inner cities. At that time, activists reacted against being unemployed and living in an impoverished state of existence, which moved into overdrive through "Thatcherism", a conservative political ideology, orchestrated by Margaret Thatcher, British Prime Minister from 1979 until 1990.

"Thatcherism" meant centralized power, competition, a free market, privatizing nationalized industries and trade union legislation, capital punishment, destroying the British manufacturing industry, mass unemployment, surging interest rates, a social housing crisis, and the privatization of the National Health Service. Ultimately it crushed and demoralized the working classes and their communities, particularly in the north of England, Wales, and Scotland. This generated a fundamental distrust of government power, and the British punk movement was the antidote that encapsulated the socioeconomic and political climate of late 1970s Britain.

SOCIAL SYSTEMS THAT MAKE HISTORY

The Smiths were the outsider's outsiders, quintessentially northern English in their outlook and approach. Their songs frequently evoked the melancholic northern landscape and working classness of the two up-two down, humdrum, industry-town architecture. It's a bitter and grim up north mentality, underpinned with unmatched intellectual wit and self-deprecating humor. They saw the unique beauty in the ugliness and the poetry in industrial architecture and the red brick factories' smoking chimneys. The Smiths influenced people's perceptions. They cultivated a fashion movement that became a pop-cultural phenomenon and cultural caricature, dressed in quiffed hairstyles, outsized blouses, faded Levi 501s, courtroom shoes, hearing aids, national health glasses, and flowers out of the backs of trousers.

They rejected the new romantic and synthesizer-based dance-pop for a modernized fusion of 1960s pop and post-punk as their own unique and distinct style. Johnny Marr's self-styled evocative and distinctive diversity of melody and mood were the unique union for this music born from the decaying industrial inner city. Morrissey had a knack to unlock the teenage psyche with his profound lyrical content and voice of reason that liberated the sexually and socially confused, ostracized youth. One of the many traits that distinguished The Smiths was they started off as self-styled pure originals, and their success was instant. Unlike all of their peers, they were good to go right out of the gate, which endured throughout their five-year existence with immense creative output and sustained influence upon music and pop culture.

SOCIAL SYSTEMS THAT MAKE HISTORY

By its own definition, The Modernist Society is a creative project and company that seeks to change people's perceptions of Modernist architecture and design by producing accessible events and products which celebrate the bold, brutal, and beautiful. It has five chapters located in Manchester, Sheffield, Leeds, Liverpool, and Birmingham, all dedicated to celebrating and engaging with twentieth-century architecture and design through publishing, events, exhibitions, and creative collaborations. Their publishing arm 'The Modernist' is a small press, publishing limited quarterly editions about 20th-century architecture and design to educate and entertain while being beautiful and engaging.

Eddy Rhead, a founding member and co-editor in chief of The Modernist magazine, said, "We were inspired by Apple Records and Factory Records' cooperative and community-centric model. They were primarily run by combining the interests of the communities they represented, with a 'Praxis'" way of, as articulated by Tony Wilson, "doing something because you have the inclination to do it and then understand why you did it after."

These independent record labels had an innovative, artist-led philosophy that fostered a culture of creativity focused on nurturing talent, which provided an alternative to the mainstream British music industry.

The Modernist has deployed a global community approach by democratizing the publishing process. It is available to all, which makes it possible for all people to understand and contribute to it from both a writing and an editorial perspective. It is a crowdsourcing model: people can self-finance it from their community of interest to achieve a cumulative result.

ANARCHY BEGINS AT HOME

Education expert Sir Ken Robinson spearheaded a radical rethink of our education systems to instill creativity as a core discipline at the grassroots and nurtured it through the educational system, instilling creative confidence because people are educated out of their creative capacity. This is because our education systems are designed to meet the bygone needs of the industrial revolution, and value recall over imagination. We benevolently steer children away from the subjects that they like because they would never get meaningful, lucrative jobs doing those things: "You are not going to be an artist, you're not going to be an actress, and you are not going to be a musician. None of these are likely to earn you money." This education system has mined our minds for a specific commodity. Sadly, this is soul-destroying advice, and is fundamentally wrong!

Many people who evolved into creative pioneers did so off their own back, not because their education system enabled them along that journey. It discouraged and ignored their difference and potential. For example, Edgar Allan Poe, Marlon Brando, Salvador Dalí, and John Lennon were expelled from school because of their indifference and because they challenged the system. Creativity is the core of humanity. Breaking rules is what creativity involves, and the rebellious nature of the mind is a catalyst to create. That does not mean breaking the law; it means questioning the status quo and treating what you do as a blank canvas to self-express and provide an alternative.

ANARCHY BEGINS AT HOME

Upbringing and genetics are obviously key to shaping our outlook. Parents need to allow children to be themselves. Being overprotected by parents drives risk-adversity, difficulty making decisions, dealing with hardship and other frustrations of life, and ultimately threatening success in life. Early specialization, tiger parenting, micromanaging children's lives, over-teaching, and testing, instead of giving time and space for creativity in an unstructured way, are the enemies of free thought and innovation.

People like Muhammad Ali, Björk, Coco Chanel, George Lucas, Leonardo da Vinci, Frank Lloyd Wright, and Walt Disney were classic outliers who had no attachment to fixed definitions of any form of life or reality, which is why they became truly great in their chosen fields. They were self-defined, self-educated, magical artists. They surprised and excited us. We are attracted to their originality and magnetic genius, encouraging us to expect the unexpected and, ultimately, to be entertained by them and to learn more about ourselves and the world we live in.

ANARCHY
BEGINS AT
HOME

Like artists, athletes are performers, and connect deeply with their audiences, in the form of fans who feel for what they do. Just as a musician sings words to us through songs, we value their creative genius because they do things most people can only dream of doing. We gush over what they do. Just like a method actor, it's what we don't see that makes the difference— the hard work, practice, and persistence to perfect their craft and achieve greatness.

Athletic greats like Pelé, George Best, Davie Cooper, Diego Maradona, and Eric Cantona were gifted with an extraordinary soccer talent that equated art with technique. Like creatives, their audience perceived them as artists and geniuses through their exceptional technical ability and creative talent that propelled them to the summit of their athletic prowess. They were renowned for their vision, passion, intelligence, quick–thinking, flair, and eye for a goal with powerful and accurate striking ability.

WHO DARES,
WINS

Compelling visions draw people in. High-performing teams are self-organizing; the performance emerges from the experts' joint actions within the project. They share a vision and commitment to the mission at hand. Similarly, the most innovative teams mobilize themselves in response to unexpected changes; they don't need a leader to tell them what to do. People who have the expertise and passion will step up at the right time in the creative process to lead and drive the completion of their respective input and add value to the team and solution. The creative atmosphere cultivated provides autonomy and space, is liberal, inclusive, and meritocratic, yet is entirely focused and motivated to expedite the mission. No hierarchy, politics, prejudice, and hangers-on are permitted or tolerated. It starts with a big idea and a shared vision; then the team works through the details to come up with the big picture.

WHO DARES, WINS

Like the British Special Air Service (SAS), the Navy SEALs are forged by adversity, endurance, and sacrifice and are key in carrying out some of the most dangerous combat and reconnaissance missions. They operate with agility in a decentralized command model. Everyone is expected to lead and be led, shunning old hierarchies (with their bad habits and lazy complacency) replacing them with modern thinking, agility, networks, and ecosystems of truly empowered teams, which improve engagement and retention and can achieve extraordinary results in pursuit of making the impossible possible.

Peak performance is a mindset that shapes what you do and how in your pursuit of excellence and self-actualization. This is done by committing to being your best every single day by performing to the maximum of your ability and seeing challenges as opportunities to continuously learn and grow. Peak performers have a global view in mind and commit to their mission by making sacrifices—long hours of training and developing mental toughness skills are worth the price for success.

Endurance Athlete Steven Wedderburn has an insatiable appetite for pushing his mental and physical capacity to the limits as a serial participant in endurance sports: Ironman Triathlons, marathons, ultramarathons, triathlons, duathlons, Gran Fondos, and cross-country ski races.

His technique involves three key steps: 1) Prepare—Train, diet, condition, speed work, train, visualization, reviewing the course, weather forecasts, and training to combat these scenarios. 2) Perform—Stick to your race strategy and trust your training, 3) Recover—diet, rest, and conduct active recovery through easy exercise.

WHO DARES,
WINS

"I visualize the entire race and set a plan for all the scenarios I anticipate for the likes of hydration, fuel, and mental toughness. Fitness is only about 40% of the formula; you need to connect the heart and mind to become a true animal by visualizing the event in advance and to train when you're tired or hungry to build resilience to the point where the mind rules the body. Developing your race strategy encompasses multiple scenarios, many of which are out of your control, that you can rapidly adapt to in the face of adversity, such as; the weather, getting injured, and getting a puncture on your bike. Because you have mental highs and lows throughout the race, you need to recognize those thought patterns when they arrive and then use them to your advantage by learning how to embrace and enjoy pain. That's what will make you achieve peak performance. Ninety-nine percent of people stop or slow down when it becomes uncomfortable. I've learned to enjoy physical and mental suffering while exercising. When you feel physically and mentally exhausted – train your mind to break through these barriers when everything else is telling you not to."

I observed a former Navy Sea, Air, and Land (SEAL) telling their story about what it was like to be a Navy SEAL. To paraphrase, one of them provided an analogy that he could get a call at 8pm tonight outlining his assignment brief, which could entail being deployed to a designation to dismantle three atom bombs. At that point, they may know nothing about the job at hand. By the time they board their flight the following morning, they have become an expert because there is a rapid learning process and the ability to tap into a broad network of highly skilled experts to provide specialist know-how and accurately inform and accelerate the learning process.

WHO DARES, WINS

A Navy SEAL knows where to look, what questions to ask, and how to pay attention to the fine details to form their approach, amid the realities of putting it into practice with mental toughness and persistence. It's about being creative on your feet by thinking and adapting to change quickly, given that you are subjected to navigating extreme adversity, ambiguity, and physically punishing activities, extremes of temperature, mental fatigue, and sleep deprivation.

There are scenarios and situations where you are given a huge amount of information, so you have to go through it rapidly to assess and understand, prioritize, decide on the strategy and tactics, and the plan forward. The other scenario is that you have limited data and need to be creative to make something out of nothing.

Sir Matt Busby managed Manchester United Football Club, Bill Shankly OBE—Liverpool, Jock Stein CBE most notably managed Celtic, and Sir Alex Ferguson famously managed Aberdeen then Manchester United. All four came from similarly industrious Scottish upbringings with a supernatural ability to build teams that made history by shaping them through their own image. They created teams with a relentless winning mindset, which resulted in an endurable, triumphant, trophy-laden dominance and resounding athletic success. They had unprecedented staying power by maintaining control over high-performing team members, an uncanny sense and eye for observation, and an ability to stay a step ahead of their contemporaries by constantly innovating and adapting to change, remaining relevant and at the top of their game.

WHO DARES,
WINS

Sports teams like the Barcelona, Bayern Munich, Brazil, Juventus, Liverpool, Manchester United, New Zealand All Blacks, and Real Madrid have created a self-sustaining winning mindset and value system through athletic excellence. The sum of the team is better than any individual. It is essential to achieve peak performance by providing the conditions for success and the autonomy and flexibility to perform.

Of course, you need talent and technical excellence in your craft to perform at what you do, but achieving greatness is more than that. It is about having the relentless intensity and focus, desire, resilience, and persistence to never give up and to achieve the highest levels of greatness.

It starts with self-belief and a desire to change your mindset. Recognizing that failure is essential to mastery. Embrace challenges, persist when confronted with setbacks, continuously learn, and keep moving forward to pursue excellence and self-actualization.

FUTURE OF
WORK

Creativity will continue to be the difference humans make in the future. Intelligent technologies are increasingly able to expedite the majority of roles a human can. The future workplace is where humans will work in unison with artificial intelligence or the technological equivalent. Robots have already multiplied productivity and replaced humans in many work lines, just as the automobile replaced horses, dramatically impacting life and society. A plane can be flown without a pilot, cars and trains driven without a driver, brain surgery without a doctor, fleets of vehicles produced without factory workers. Freeing up humans to perform more creative and self-fulfilling roles that have yet to be defined.

There will be an all-encompassing gig economy, where people will have multiple gigs simultaneously, on a part-time or full-time capacity with a single company, or a variety of employers at the same time. This will drive the need to be a true expert in your craft, and ultimately help minimize the hindrances, barriers, and toxicity that can get in the way of making the work happen. Many organizations are still glued to the past, managing in classic functional and operational ways designed for mass-produced, manufactured, one size fits all, industrial revolution organizational systems.

FUTURE OF
WORK

Within the digital revolution, organizations need to be designed based on speed, agility, and adaptation to the modern age, business, and how work gets done. High-performing teams are usually self-organizing. The performance emerges from the experts' joint actions within the project, sharing a vision that they commit to the purpose and the mission. Similarly, the most innovative teams mobilize themselves in response to unexpected changes. They don't need a leader to tell them what to do.

The purpose of organizational development is to provide leading-edge thinking, practice, and programs. Dave Gartenberg has been at the forefront of the human resources profession for over 30 years, from economic analyst and teaching fellow to various executive HR leaderships (including Chief People Officer) at companies like Microsoft, Avanade, and Slalom. He has captained all aspects of human resource management, industrial relations policies, practices, and operations. Dave provides perspective on organizational effectiveness and culture transformation to accelerate innovation and optimize business performance.

"One of the most pivotal stories I've heard was from a business leader that I supported earlier in my career," says Dave. "He was part of a major project where they shipped the product to the wrong location, costing the company $25 million to fix it. It was clearly a mistake he was responsible for, so he went to the CEO to hand in his resignation. He openly admitted what he did and what he did to fix it. The CEO's response was literally priceless: 'I just invested $25 million in your development, and I'm pretty sure you're not going to make that mistake again!'" How many organizations do you think would actually pull that off? How many CEOs would do something like that? Not a lot! The point is that it's okay to fail if it's a teachable moment and wasn't done out of arrogance or ignorance. A culture of thinking, learning, and

doing is instilled within values and behaviors, and it starts from the top and let it bleed and flow from there.
 from there."

The leadership tone and value system need to be set at the top of an organization to encourage continuous learning by developing knowledge and competence, resulting in employee growth and business success.

Dave has experimented with and applied several models to help shape culture strategy and optimize organizational excellence, with The Star Model by Jay Galbraith being one of the more prominent approaches.

"The model consists of five areas connected and aligned to help shape the decisions and behaviors of an organization: Strategy, Structure, Processes, Rewards, and People," says Dave. "The business model is at the core of the star, operating as the heartbeat distributing the DNA across all areas. The organization takes a holistic view in the direction the company wants to go."

This system-thinking approach takes a holistic view of how structures, patterns, and cycles within systems all fit together, rather than just seeing the specific parts or a polarized view of the system.

From building brands in Brazil and the USA, Leticia Pettená has dedicated herself to changing behavior for the better by influencing corporate cultures and societies through strategic focus, creative thinking, and technology innovation, helping the likes of Itaú, Natura, IBM, Nestlé, Rise Ventures, Beleaf, Verde Asset Management, and Beautybox to reimagine their brands.

"Listening to input from society can tell us about what they truly

FUTURE OF
WORK

want to experience from the brands that we design for," says Leticia. "It is critical to approach this with an open mind and childlike wonder without preconceptions and biases getting in the way so as to reboot your mind to being in an uninterrupted starting place with a fresh perspective."

Effective prioritization and focusing on what truly matters to find the truth behind a brand that people actually believe in, then how that can be evoked within the brand design so that people are at the heart of the purpose, that they feel connected to something greater, feel good and confident, and trust the brand.

When a brand connects emotionally to its consumers by providing authentic, personalized, and unique experiences, the alchemy happens. Brand love is created by establishing trust, and making people feel good, confident, and connected to something greater.

Business executive Steven Harris has led complex international operations and implemented strategic change in the pharmaceutical, oil and gas, and manufacturing industries. "Creativity has to have value and progressive output, or it's just another thought or random action. Effective prioritization and selection of innovative ideas are worked through within specific business contexts that impact the bottom line. Examples include accelerating innovation, enabling growth, optimizing productivity, or mitigating costs and removing operational inefficiencies. Using standard approaches and methods helps plan and expedite the transformation and culture change needed while managing innovation to gain a return on the investment. Soliciting insight from data to understand needs, concerns, priorities, expectations, market and competitive trends, and forces drives change. Once the idea has been evaluated and prioritized, some become a strategic initiative, whether a new or an existing enhancement to

FUTURE OF
WORK

a product or service, aligning the culture, setting the right leadership tone, and making the resources available to bring the initiative to life. Ultimately, it is all about people, focus and execution, and if you don't have that well-oiled and good to go, it is unlikely to succeed."

This approach is about finding the nexus between creativity and commerciality using qualitative and quantitative measures to balance risk with reward to drive business innovation and outcomes.

From Virgin to Rough Trade, Play It Again Sam (PIAS), and Grand Royal Records, then Trust Management to guiding the careers of hundreds of revered artists who have influenced popular culture (The Beastie Boys to Johnny Marr, Ash, We Are Scientists, Dexys, and Baxter Dury), working with artists who have received Ivor Novello Awards, Oscar nominations, and New Musical Express (NME) Godlike Genius Awards, and mentoring the next generation of artists, producers, and entrepreneurs at the Academy of Contemporary Music, Dave Cronen's creative philosophy is about having a strong work ethic and do-it-yourself sensibility in the spirit of "the harder you work, the luckier you get."

Whether shaping artists' careers, booking gigs, planning album projects, orchestrating record releases and tours, creating marketing and merchandising strategies, or ensuring artists get paid for their work, the DIY sensibility is critical in how you approach your work. Pulling up your sleeves and just doing it, combined with a strong work ethic, are the must-haves because you've got the responsibility of managing someone else's career, over and above your own, and that comes with serious responsibility, persistence, and care, often resulting in doing whatever it takes to make things happen and get them over the line.

FUTURE OF
WORK

"When we did *The Only Way Is Up* by Yazz and the Plastic Population, it became a smash hit in the United Kingdom and the second best-selling single of that year," says Dave. "We were literally sitting on the sidewalk of the warehouse at Rough Trade's Collier Street Headquarters in London, putting the 7" vinyl records we'd just received from the manufacturer into record sleeves we'd received from the printers.

We spent hours putting them together to get 50,000 units shipped every few days at its peak to the record stores. There have been countless stories like this that I've been involved with, such as The Smiths, Depeche Mode, and KLF." Dave continued, "It was a constant elating feeling that equated the belief in the ingenuity of the artists' music with being part of a skilled, diverse, and committed team drawn together by a unified energy and common purpose for the greater good by bringing their art to market, which had a direct impact upon popular culture and musical history."

Fostering a creative culture means having a strong sense of acceptance, belonging, and connection to a greater purpose and whole. You feel safe, valued, and empowered, with ownership of what you do and how you do it. Your cultural identity is shaped by the values and attitudes internal and external to the world you live in, the people you engage with, and the activities you do. To achieve self-actualization, it is important to keep moving forward and experimenting with and trying out new experiences by maintaining a current and modernist mindset and having a global and holistic view, which will help you solve problems with an open mind and more innovatively, overcoming prejudice and having more diverse and better ideas. When a culture loses touch with its creativity, it becomes insulated and imprisoned, and people become closed-minded, culturally oppressive, and lost in time and life.

6

AESTHETICS IN LOVE: THE CREATIVE PROCESS

AESTHETICS IN LOVE: THE CREATIVE PROCESS

The creative process initiates and transforms an idea into actualization by bringing it to fruition through three steps—Dream, Make, and Do. Supported by true stories and perspectives from creative industry experts about their creative processes, keys to success, and pitfalls to avoid.

MAGIC TAKES
PLANNING

Every single creative will tell you that there is no on and off button for creativity. It is a constant that happens naturally, by design, or by accident in our everyday lives. Though the creative process may seem magical, especially where ideas can come from and how they are brought to form and life, there are proven techniques, tools, methods, frameworks, and approaches to the art and science of applied creativity that make it happen.

What it does not mean is being fooled into believing that it is simply about following a process and expecting creative results as an outcome. It is all about people and the execution, because people with a vision combined with passion and drive make things happen. To pursue your idea with conviction and resilience, be skilled in your craft and expedite quality precision to bring your idea to life. Have true grit to slay the naysayers, push through adversity and ambiguity with leadership, make sacrifices, and execute your ideas in a disciplined way.

The creative process is about making new connections between past and present ideas, and infusing economic, political, sociocultural, and technological perspectives in parallel to produce new business models, products, services, or experiences. The steps in the process involve discovering and developing insights, involving divergent thinking to analyze a problem, generating and evaluating ideas that can become concepts, experimenting, prototyping, constructing, and making a plan of action.

MAGIC TAKES
PLANNING

Creative thinking is the ability to look at the same thing as everybody else but see something different. It encompasses divergent thinking, perceiving patterns that are not obvious, creating and expressing art through a concept, method, solution, design, work of art, or physical object. It applies techniques that drive evolution, synthesis, re-application, reinvention, reimagination, disruption, revolution, and changing direction.

How do we find creativity? Do we simply dream up ideas from within ourselves, what we manifest from what we observe and the world we live in, or do ideas fall from the sky, and gravitate toward us?

Being principle-led helps drive clarity on what is important to you. It will align you to what matters, reflecting your values and tastes, which will ultimately lead you to create a unique artistic identity that is aesthetically pleasing to you, acting as a moral compass on what you do and how.

The five principles of creativity are imagination, innovation, aesthetics, entrepreneurship, and manifestation. Dream, make, and do, are the three phases of the creative process. The process is iterative and constant, and customizable per craft, situation, and opportunity.

The five principles for creativity are:

Principles

1 IMAGINATION

Create, design, and make new things with childlike imagination and discovery by seeing the unseen and navigating the journey to get there by evoking magic and delight, dreaming up what doesn't exist, and turning your imagination into art.

2 INNOVATION

Dream up and bring novel ideas to life in a practical form. This can be infused in products, services, or experiences, which create commercial value or positive societal benefits. Revel in finding the future by tinkering with and experimenting with technologies and cross-pollinating across multiple domains in the creative arts and beyond to make art that adds value.

3 AESTHETIC

Blend art and science with excellence in craftsmanship by anticipating future trends inspired by culture and aesthetics connected to emotions and imagination. Be minimal in the spirit of less is more by concentrating on the essentials only. Let your craftsmanship be laser-focused to the last detail because care and accuracy show mindfulness and respect for your audience.

4 ENTREPRENEURIALISM

Fearlessly lead toward invisible horizons by applying a do-it-yourself sensibility to finding the future by being adaptive, persistent, and resilient in bringing new solutions to market. Be independent-minded and self-sufficient from start to finish, always finding the alternative by rejecting the banal and status quo in your own voice and style.

5 MANIFESTATION

Light the way into the future by taking "what is not" and making it "what can be" by bringing meaning to the humdrum and breaking through conventional values, tastes, and perceptions. Connect emotionally with people across every culture and walk of life worldwide, making it relatable and understandable by providing purpose and meaning.

creativity

The Creative Process

Ideas only change things by doing the work. This approach originates and brings ideas to actualization by creating new and original products, services, or experiences that have commercial and societal value.

It is about discovering and developing insight, involving divergent thinking to analyze a problem, generating ideas, constructing and critiquing a plan of action to bring it to life. The three phases are dream, make, and do. In the FIRST phase think as an outsider with childlike imagination and wonder, to gain an analytical, external view of the challenge. Then dream purposeful breakthrough ideas and brainstorm ideal solutions without frontiers to find the future.

Use divergent thinking to conceive creative and radical ideas. In the SECOND phase adopt a maker mindset. Using convergent thinking to review and select best ideas, rapidly prototype and construct a plan. The THIRD phase is that of doing with agility. Review the solution in order to identify improvements, obstacles, or risks. Improve the solution then rigorously execute and make it real by bringing it all together and activate impactfully with desired audiences and markets. The sequence is iterative and constant.

Idea   Actualized

● Mystery
● Tension

1 DREAM	**2** MAKE	**3** DO
Imagine the impossible by making the invisible visible	Take what is not and make it what is by applying a Do-It-Yourself sensibility to create and craft	Produce solutions that add commercial and societal value

The Creative Process
Dream. Make. Do.

CONNECT PAST TO PRESENT

Economics

WHAT TO DO
BUSINESS
PRODUCT
SERVICE
EXPERIENCE

Politics

Technology

Socio-culture

HOW TO DO IT
DREAM
MAKE
DO

LIGHT THE WAY INTO FUTURE

DREAM — Imagine the impossible by making the invisible visible

MAKE — Take what is not and make it what is by applying a Do-It-Yourself sensibility to create and craft

DO — Produce solutions that add commercial and societal value

TURNING YOUR IDEAS INTO ART

The Three Phases of the Creative Process

Dream: The first phase is about imagining the impossible by making the invisible visible; you have to think as an outsider with childlike imagination and wonder to gain an analytical and external view of the challenge. Apply divergent thinking to dream without frontiers to find the breakthrough ideas by envisioning the desired outcome. As you navigate your creative journey, prepare for what needs to be done and generate ideas by gathering resources and researching to find a breakthrough idea. Envision the art of the possible by setting your mind free, fostering divergent thinking to explore all possible approaches to developing your vision. Freeing your brain tends to apply its own experiences from your mental reservoir of thoughts, expertise, and instincts by drawing on insight, know-how, and past experiences to dream up novel ideas. Then remove yourself from the idea to seek broader perspectives and take a more integrative approach before honing it further.

TURNING YOUR IDEAS INTO ART

Make: In the second phase, take what is not and make it by applying a do-it-yourself sensibility using convergent thinking to review and select the best ideas and then rapidly prototype and construct the plan to bring it to life. Validating your idea against alternatives allow your solution to align with your vision. For example, as an entrepreneur or business leader, this will typically entail researching the idea's hypothesis, such as your business model's viability and technology feasibility. Depending on the results, it may involve having to rethink, rip it up and start again, or soldiering forward with the wind firmly in your sails, clear and assured by what you're doing..

Do: The third phase is getting it done by turning ideas into solutions. Review the solution to identify improvements, make eliminations, fine-tune, remove obstacles, mitigate risks, and bring it to life with your audience and markets, whether your solution is a new business, brand campaign, a physical product, an industrial design, song, film, story or painting. Finalize the solution and bring it to market by activating all relevant distribution platforms and channels.

TURNING YOUR IDEAS INTO ART

This creative process blends the art and science of creativity by balancing creative thinking to create, interpret, and express art with critical thinking to explore an opportunity or problem, define and test a hypothesis, and answer questions.

Anticipate future trends inspired by industry developments, culture, and aesthetics connected to emotions, imagination, and elegantly composed artistic solutions. These are structured within a cohesive and proven framework that combines qualitative and quantitative research methods, practical insights, and techniques, informing, framing, and guiding the choices you make, either individually or collaboratively, between self-organizing multidisciplinary teams, start-up businesses, and large organizations. Generate ideas, develop concepts, and bring them to market efficiently.

These ideas are supported by unique perspectives and practical applications from the creative industry experts whom I interviewed about their approaches to creativity in their respective domains and disciplines, including actors, art directors, artists, branders, creative directors, curators, entrepreneurs, designers, filmmakers, illustrators, marketers, musicians, photographers, producers, and product developers.

Dream

1 ENVISIONING
It starts with a dream full of passion and enthusiasm, without any restrictions or criticism. This stage's purpose is to generate, develop, and communicate new ideas that challenge the status quo. "Imagine if…", "What if…?"

2 SEARCH TO DISCOVER
Find and discover relevant topics and deeply understand them by listening, discussing, and visualizing through reflection, sketching, or storyboarding.

3 MENTORSHIP
Engage with and solicit input from industry experts, and immerse yourself in the domain.

4 STAND ON THE SHOULDERS OF GIANTS AND LEARN FROM THE GREATS
Use existing knowledge by learning from pioneers of the past and build upon their innovations rather than reinventing the wheel.

5 MARKET RESEARCH
Define the research challenges, questions, and the methodology to address them. Assess the market forces driving change from an economic, political, sociocultural, and technological perspective. Identify industry standards and best practices. Synthesize insights to set future trends and opportunities.

6 FORECASTING TRENDS
Proactively explore trends and determine future scenarios that anticipate market shifts by identifying changes in tastes and preferences.

7 CREATIVE STRATEGY
Synthesize research, evaluate insights, and refine your best ideas. Formulate and communicate creative strategy, resulting in brand cohesion and integrity across all touchpoints.

8 STORYTELLING
Build audience-specific narratives and storytelling themes that spark awareness, build perception, generate demand and drive brand reputation.

9 PRINCIPLES
Create and direct creative principles that turn ideas into artistic concepts and expressions that are actionable.

10 CREATIVE DIRECTION
Define creative direction that drives cohesion and brand experience and flow across all touchpoints.

11 POSITIONING
Establish a creative framework, informed by market and audience research, to guide solution decisions that differentiate from the competition.

12 EXPERIMENTATION
Experiment, prototype, and learn by doing in a social environment by sharing ideas, skills, and resources across multiple domains.

13 ASSET CREATION
Design and direct the aesthetic direction by creating assets that foster an emotional connection with audiences.

14 CONCEPTUAL MODELLING
Apply the design-based people-centered approach to synthesize audience perspectives that differentiate.

Make

15 PROTOTYPING
Rapidly prototype and communicate solution concepts, narratives, and value proposition that embody the intended audience's values, are defensible in the marketplace, and are an authentic expression of brand values.

16 CO-CREATION
Develop new concepts, solutions, products, and services with experts, consumers, partners, and community interaction and knowledge. Solicit input, share information, and exchange ideas collectively to improve the outputs.

17 INCUBATION
Continuously improve the design through elimination and refinement, informed by research, across all aspects of the solution.

18 TECHNOLOGY TRANSFER
Apply new technology innovations that create market opportunities to commercialize products.

19 PRODUCT & SERVICE DESIGN
Translate insights from an audience, commercial, and technical perspectives from all relevant sources and infuse them into the solution design.

20 PRODUCT & SERVICE DEVELOPMENT
Ensure quality completeness of the entire product or service that optimizes the audience's experience and realizes the potential value.

21 PRODUCT & SERVICE LIFECYCLE MANAGEMENT
Implement infrastructure and support systems to enable the successful launch of the product or service.

Do

22 **GO TO MARKET**
Bring to market the unique value proposition across all relevant channels efficiently and to maximize return on investment.

23 **PRICING**
Conduct market research and apply business modeling tools and techniques to define pricing that differentiates from competitors and maximizes investment return.

24 **DISTRIBUTION**
Prioritize and activate the right distribution channels that bring the solution to target audiences effectively.

25 **COMMUNICATIONS**
Activate communication vehicles, such as public relations and digital media, across owned, earned, and paid marketing channels.

26 **MEASUREMENT**
Measure commercial impact and infuse insights into learnings that drive continuous improvement and innovation.

HOW THE SOUL FOR MAKING ART WORKS

Johnny Marr has spent the last four decades blending the art and science of his craft as a musical pioneer by connecting to the chords of our soul, influencing popular culture, inspiring thousands of musicians, and affecting millions of people's lives through his music.

I spent two glorious summer days with Johnny, in his industrial-chic converted factory studio in Manchester to produce the documentary *Creativity in the Digital Age*, about his creative process, why sustained creativity is a true differentiator, and how he has been able to regularly break through the status quo and embolden others to do the same by becoming a role model for true ingenuity.

Johnny says, "From the minute I could string a few chords together, I always saw playing an instrument as the pursuit of greatness. I use the guitar as a tool to make something artistic. We had a couple of producers in the early days, and I just watched those guys like a hawk, and, in some ways, there were a couple of characters who became mentors to me. I was like a sponge trying to learn everything I could from these older people." Marr recorded every idea because he never knew what the idea was going to turn into. His approach to learning was to learn from doing. "How to make a record was just to roll my sleeves up and pretend that I was able to do it." Changes in technology influenced the way he worked through experimentation and bringing his ideas to life: "Imagination and the human heart and the human spirit, which is the thing that goes into those ones and zeros, and manipulates them, sometimes, brilliantly, and sometimes accidentally, into a piece of work that the other humans can react to."

HOW THE SOUL FOR MAKING ART WORKS

Marr paid homage to his strong work ethic and doer ethos through Picasso's motto that: "Inspiration exists, but it has to find you working."

Embracing originality and making unique connections between disparate universes to light the way into the future; "The idea of feeling like you never know enough is an inspiring concept, and collaboration is a useful trigger for new experiences and inspiration."

Stanley Kubrick shot millions of reels of film, knowing that most of it would end up on the cutting room floor. He assembled and refined different pieces to create a cohesive whole, which shows that the creative process can be half inspiration and half elimination. Martin Scorsese is infamous for his gritty and meticulously detailed filmmaking style. Quentin Tarantino has repeatedly exploited B movies and pop culture history to pay homage, instead of shamelessly plagiarizing them, as a token of respect for the past. He connects it to the present in his moviemaking approach. Steven Spielberg is committed to never resting on his laurels and cashing in. He constantly makes progress by making new material, applying the latest techniques and technologies while ensuring his movies are of the moment and engaging and appeal to all audiences regardless of demographics and ages.

HOW THE SOUL FOR MAKING ART WORKS

From BBC Television to Hollywood movie director, Golden Globe nominee and British Academy of Film and Television Arts (BAFTA) award winner, to collaborator with Martin Scorsese, Danny Boyle, Jim Carrey, Mick Jagger and a host of award-winning actors, filmmaker Jon S. Baird is not one for improvising. He always has a plan. He treats the script as his Bible and never puts anything into production until it is solid. He takes the time to get everything right with the script before moving into the pre-production process. Organizing the right crew for the right job is crucial. "The most experienced people are not necessarily the best for this job. People who are most passionate about the script understand the story and bring their particular skills to the genre film, which is important. That's a big part of the planning process," he says. For example, storyboarding involves having a script and being lucky enough to work with a budget that allows the involvement of a visual concept artist, someone to bring it to life, to give the entire crew an idea of what is in their head. Moving forward, choosing the actors, choosing locations, and planning a film is years in the making; the film's shooting is the shortest part of the process. In Jon's own words, "Shooting a movie may take seven to ten weeks—that's the short part. The pre-production, however, is years in the making. Sometimes, the post-production and editing can be a huge beast; it's another year as well. So, in a nutshell, the more planning, the more creativity there is on set. Falling back on a plan doesn't mean that everything needs to be according to plan. There is room for improvisation. My advice to people would be to put the time in at the beginning. Everything's in the plan."

Jon has always been mindful and selective in what he has done and with whom, as well as a flawless planner, organizer, networker, and natural leader of people. He is a determined, single-minded person of action with an insatiable drive and ambition to make things happen through focus, dedication, and hard work.

HOW THE SOUL FOR MAKING ART WORKS

Some people, by contrast, let themselves get flushed by hopeless pessimism and self-doubt. They allow themselves to feel unintelligent, ineffective, and incapable of achievement, cave under pressure, and give up in the face of setbacks. They do not see obstacles as opportunities to reach new heights of achievement through hard work and perseverance, nor do they learn quickly from failure by improving their skills.

Jon has a knack for living in the present, believing in himself, being self-disciplined, making himself accountable for his actions, being resilient and positive when faced with setbacks and adversity, and being open-minded by redefining these situations as a process for learning and growing.

Traveling through America and tasting the magic of Hollywood led Ben Thornley down the path he has since excelled in— creating inspirational content for delivery over a global platform with thousands of clients from Madagascar's rainforests to Mumbai's streets, where his films have been viewed by over a billion people. His team typically starts with a song to envision what the video will be.

If someone pitches an idea and the budget covers it, he then says, "we would go away and brainstorm after that initial conversation and just try and come up with as many ideas as possible. Get as many ideas on the board as possible. Then we go through them with a fine-tooth comb and figure out what's doable and what's not doable and just nail that down into work. Ideally, there should be a single page treatment; a single page has the kind of information that works well in a music video."

HOW THE
SOUL FOR
MAKING ART
WORKS

Actress Cathy Murphy, who has gone from being a student at the Sylvia Young Theatre School to Allan Clarke's *Made in Britain*, *Stars of the Roller Skate Disco*, *Doctor Who*, *EastEnders*, *Holby City*, *Family Affairs*, *The Phantom of the Opera*, *Shameless*, *Extras*, *About A Boy*, *Misery*, *Two Woman*, *Once A Catholic* and many more, says about the creative process,

"You have to find your own way as an actor by crafting and formulating the right techniques and methods that work for you. Know your craft, always come prepared, and bring your own unique perspective to the character, whether that's through voice, style, look, hair, dress, walk, or the way you hold yourself, which can add to a character. For example, when I played the antagonist Annie Wilkes in the West End-stage adaptation of *Misery*, I tried to depict her complex persona, representing her paranoid bipolar character by oscillating interchangeably between her cheery deceptive façade and her malicious intent and sinister behavior."

Method acting was adopted by actors like Marlon Brando, Al Pacino, Robert De Niro, and Daniel Day-Lewis to emotionally self-identify with the character and fully immerse themselves in a role.

Daniel Day-Lewis infamously prepared for his roles in excruciating detail by experiencing the lives and feelings of the characters he played, often going to extreme dedication. He learned how to write and paint with his feet, spent weeks in a clinic to deeply connect with the condition of cerebral palsy in *My Left Foot*. Spent time in solitary confinement with no food or *water for In the Name of the Father*. Learned how to build canoes, fight with tomahawks, skinned and cooked animals for *The Last of the Mohicans*.

HOW THE SOUL FOR MAKING ART WORKS

Radio and podcast broadcasting are "the theater of the mind". It does not have any visual or physical representation of what is occurring. It leaves an audience to conjure up its own mental images of what the words and conversation uniquely mean to them by connecting to the chords of their souls.

Content marketer and CEO of creative agency and production studio Feelr Media Jonathan Keith says, "the creative process is not something that you turn on or off; it is always on. We are surrounded by inspiring and interesting stories in our everyday lives. As humans, we have a primal sense and antenna to self-navigate and orientate. By sensing, touching, feeling, and seeing around the corners, we seek inspiration, capture new ideas, and generate compelling stories across many reference points and domains, and make those connections real by bringing them to life through solutions and experiences that engage and excite."

This approach is based on being constantly tuned in to the world around and within you in everyday life. It also entails proactively researching, observing, challenging, and forming a perspective on industry developments, culture, and aesthetics, as well as identifying patterns and relationships, connecting them to the emotions and imagination, and manifesting this into purposeful solutions.

HOW THE
SOUL FOR
MAKING ART
WORKS

Co-founder of Loaded Pictures and executive producer Brian Homman operates as the creative bridge between brands and his talented multidisciplinary team by overseeing all aspects of video production, motion design, animation, and branded content across a diverse range of clients from Microsoft, T-Mobile, Fox Sports, MTV, and McDonald's to Pizza Hut, AT&T, and the Bill & Melinda Gates Foundation. "Have a voracious appetite for information, learning, and history as it all comes together in your work," says Brian.

Having insatiable curiosity and a hunger for knowledge and continuous self-improvement by studying the greats and learning from the past, building upon history by not reinventing the wheel, being eclectic in your work, and operating with integrity to show the traceability of ideas and reference points is key. A case in point: Talent does not borrow, and geniuses do not steal?

Freelance executive producer Scott Reid has overseen multiple media productions by working independently to orchestrate script development, directing, and editing at the BBC, Sky, and STV. He says, "Imagination has no frontiers. Creativity is seeing what others don't, or until it is presented to them. It often means turning an everyday observation and situation into something entertaining, engaging, funny, sad, and attractive for an audience, or creating a new perspective or novel pathway for how the audience considers the product, service, or experience." says Scott. "Ideas come from where and when you least expect, especially when you are relaxed and free from pressure, time constraints, structured processes, and stifled environments. Never stop yourself from considering any idea. A so-called bad idea can have one nugget of insight that can generate a spark that makes the idea into a bigger and better one."

HOW THE
SOUL FOR
MAKING ART
WORKS

Scott's approach uses brainstorming as a vehicle to apply divergent thinking to initiate and develop ideas from many different people regardless of their field of expertise. Don't get fooled into believing that creatives are the only source of good ideas. Rather, engagement across multiple fields and backgrounds can provide novel perspectives and drive new thinking and ideas.

Authentic photographers are artists who use the camera as a wand to blend their artistic eye with technical know-how to capture snapshots in time. Photography is a visual language that expresses their imagination, beauty, emotions, and time. As the advertising executive Fred R. Barnard said, "one look is worth a thousand words".

Photographer Jill Furmanovsky has taken pictures of some of the greatest musicians of all time, including Led Zeppelin, The Rolling Stones, Madness, Debbie Harry, Pink Floyd, Oasis, Bob Dylan, Joy Division, Queen, Tom Waits, Chrissie Hynde, The Clash, Björk, and Amy Winehouse. "The creative process is not easy. It doesn't always flow. You have to be very persistent, make wrong turns, and often fail before you get to something precious," says Jill. "It is magical, mysterious, and difficult to define. It's largely instinctive where it feels like you are magnetically drawn toward specific things and repelled by others. There is communication between yourself, the camera, and the object. You have to clear your head to see with clarity."

HOW THE SOUL FOR MAKING ART WORKS

Brian Smale has photographed some of the world's leading businessmen and women, scientists, inventors, and politicians. He has had assignments for magazines such as *Fortune, BusinessWeek, Forbes, Fast Company, Esquire, GQ, Rolling Stone,* and *Spin.* His commercial clients include Microsoft, Panasonic, Boeing, Fuji, and Seattle Children's Hospital. "The purpose of a photography assignment is to capture the essence of the subject and make it memorable. With editorial assignments, you tend to get a description of the personality and story," he says. "I then start plotting out the shoot by researching and familiarizing myself with the subject. If it is simply a portrait that is needed, I'll try to get an idea of what possibilities exist for relevant situations or locations to shoot in. In these cases, I try not to be too wedded to an actual visual in advance, since reality is usually a lot different than what is in your imagination, and just work with what is available. If there is a more abstract concept that needs to be conveyed, then I will start to think about things that may be important to the subject, such as objects, tools, lighting, composition, or some other visual device, and try to incorporate them into the photo. Sometimes the solution comes when actively thinking about it. At other times, it will just pop into my head while I am doing something completely unrelated, like taking a shower or walking the dog. I try to write it down before it pops back out! Occasionally one needs to experiment and test an idea, but if you know your tools well and have enough time to work on them, you should succeed. Having a simpler 'Plan B' in your back pocket, just in case, is usually a good idea, too!"

An illustrator is an artist who uses their imagination to enhance the written word and expound on concepts by providing visual representation and meaning. Anita Kunz has created iconic art that has been internationally shown and published for four decades. She is famous for her covers for the New Yorker, Time Magazine, Rolling Stone, the New York Times Magazine,

HOW THE
SOUL FOR
MAKING ART
WORKS

and many others. Her work has appeared in numerous galleries and museums, and she has won many awards for it. "It always starts with an idea," she says. "There is always a kernel of an idea that is provided to me in the form of an advertisement, a manuscript, a story, or a book. For commercial illustration, it always begins with something that I interpret with an illustration as clearly as I can because I want to make an image that works in conjunction with the text, whether it agrees with the text or not. My personal work is in fine art and books, where the ideas come much more from my world experience and what I want to express, whether that has to do with honoring certain people or being politically critical. When I do client work, they typically require sketches of the work upfront, so I try to make the sketches as detailed as possible so that I don't surprise them and I try and be as professional as possible about sending sketches. Then they can choose their preferred options or provide input for me to make modifications. Then I take the idea to completion by making actual physical paintings in acrylic and watercolor. Obviously, it varies depending on what the project is. Idea generation is always first, then sketching, then the final painting. If it needs to be submitted to a client, I scan, color correct, and transmit it digitally."

Musician and producer Doviak has had many experiences, from working on high profile commercials and films to being Johnny Marr's co-producer and Melanie Isaac, Priya Panda, and Benjamin Schoos' co-writer and producer, to mixing music for multiple up-and-coming bands to being an acclaimed independent artist. His process typically starts with a basic idea, which can sometimes take shape very quickly. Occasionally, the entire song might be sketched out very quickly. But very often, that's not the case, and it can be a slow and arduous process

HOW THE
SOUL FOR
MAKING ART
WORKS

"One of the problems some people have with creativity is not knowing where to start. It's like having an entire world and spectrum of possibilities. Creativity can come from chaos, so there is a need to instill some structure into that chaos. Otherwise, it becomes hard to manage and can destroy your momentum."

Independent musician Iwan Gronow, the bassist in Johnny Marr's band, has toured the world and played at festivals including Glastonbury, Coachella, and Fuji Rock, and appeared on Later with Jools Holland and The Tonight Show with Jimmy Fallon. "It starts with a rhythm, beat, or crafting a simple chord arrangement, a melody that I've dreamed up from my imagination," Iwan says. "The key is to find the creative trigger and just start! Then, develop the musical concept organically by infusing additional instruments like guitars and synthesizers, depending on whether the song needs it. I work on the lyrics and ideas individually or with my bandmates on the song's building blocks and decide on the sonic, instrumentation, arrangements— the intro, verse, chorus, bridge, outro, recording, and production."and contributions, exactly one minute long, with no organic instruments. Like clockwork, each Monday and Wednesday, he committed to writing, recording, and producing two songs. This became a political, disciplined, and systematic approach that generated consistent and frequent output with a distinct purpose, aesthetic, and identity.

This approach is iterative and constant, encompassing idea inception, concept development, orchestration of musical talent and instrumentation, bringing it all together, and making it cohesive within a finished product brought to life through recorded and live performance.

HOW THE SOUL FOR MAKING ART WORKS

Musician and producer Iain Mutch is a maker, a doer, and a lifelong musical journeyman driven by insatiable intellectual curiosity, passion, and a thirst for experiential creative pursuits. He expands into disparate topics, experimentation, tinkering, and deepening his subject-matter expertise across time and space. He finds endless joy during the ups and downs of the creative process. He has applied various techniques inspired by Dada, William Burroughs, and David Bowie to his work. He composes work by carving up the pages as part of his creative process, taking conventional finished text and cutting it into single words, then rearranging the words into a new text. He also imposes constraints upon himself and works religiously within those parameters to drive a specific outcome.

During the COVID-19 pandemic, he established an art house project with a manifesto inspired by the situational factors influencing changing human behavior, combined with Jean-Paul Sartre's inspired existential ideas about the human spirit and life.

Each song had to be about the pandemic's human experience. They invited multiple artists to provide their lyrical perspectives and contributions, exactly one minute long, with no organic instruments. Like clockwork, each Monday and Wednesday, he committed to writing, recording, and producing two songs. This became a political, disciplined, and systematic approach that generated consistent and frequent output with a distinct purpose, aesthetic, and identity.

Professor Malcolm Garrett MBE RDI is a graphic designer who has mastered the art and science of creativity, as evidenced by a diverse portfolio that spans four decades. He has created landmark designs for musicians and bands, including Buzzcocks, Duran Duran, Simple Minds, Boy George, Peter Gabriel, Oasis, and Pulp, and done numerous innovative digital projects for

HOW THE SOUL FOR MAKING ART WORKS

clients such as Apple, Virgin, Warner Brothers, Transport for London, Christian Aid, and Design Manchester. He has also worked with publishing, film, and TV companies to reimagine their businesses through new media platforms and immersive technologies.

"Brian Eno and I had a conversation about where ideas come from. We concluded that if you wanted to have an idea, don't try and think of it, don't try and find an idea, go and do something else and the idea will find you," says Malcolm.

"There are two stages to my approach. Firstly, think about the problem in detail but think about it while doing something else, such as going to a gallery or museum, watching a film, or reading a book. These strange connections start to form, and by coming out of the problem, the solution becomes clearer. Secondly, sit down and start drawing. Because once you start drawing, all of those things you've thought about begin to influence the directions your drawings take."

Core to Malcolm's approach is the manifestation of how he feels inside and the things that he observes in everyday life, making connections from past to present, and across multiple disciplines and domains, regardless of how abstract they may appear at first, where he crystallizes the solution to a problem.

"It's all about making connections," says Malcolm. "I've learned over time that I'm as much a connector as a designer. I connect people to information, people to people, designers to designers, and clients to clients. I like to find connections between things and people. My design work and design solutions are typically a combination of two or more seemingly disconnected ideas or thoughts that appear to me could be brought together to create a third thing."

HOW THE
SOUL FOR
MAKING ART
WORKS

"The bottom line is empathy," Malcolm continued. "I've come to understand that what I do is actually never really my work. If you are designing, you are by default trying to convey something for somebody else, to somebody else, by conveying the information that belongs to that environment, to the people that need to experience it. For example, if you are designing a record sleeve, you're trying to convey the sense of the music, attitude, tone, voice, and style of the musician, and translating that to connect with an audience that wants to hear, or may not yet know that they want to hear. The better you do your job, the more invisible you as a designer become, because if you see the design, then that's interrupting the communications process. Communication just has to work without thought. For example, what do you see when you think about Pink Floyd's *The Dark Side of the Moon*? Light refracting from a triangular prism across a black background. That visual icon and the record *The Dark Side of the Moon* are inextricably linked and have thus become synonymous, and that's what a good designer does. They don't just draw a triangle with light rays that go through it—they create a sense of comprehension that transcends the imagery."

Since the mid-1990s, Graphic Designer Devon Baker has created designs for Unknown Origins, Microsoft, Centrify, McCall Hall, Verizon, Sprint, Cafe Racer TV, Clear Wireless, Dell, UW Medicine, Dime City Cycles, and Red Oxx Manufacturing.

"I treat the creative process as an epic adventure, where I'm always accompanied by a soundtrack while navigating open waters because music inspires my thinking and the way I work," says Devon. "I try not to set too many parameters because I don't want to limit myself in the art of the possible and want to avoid making the process stagnant. Sometimes you'll run aground; the key is to never give up because that perfect concept and its execution are just around the bend. Don't judge how you work creatively, be unapologetically bold by fearlessly throwing your line out there; you know when you've nailed it. To catch the big fish is the prize, but having fun throughout the

HOW THE
SOUL FOR
MAKING ART
WORKS

process is the best reward."

Design pioneer Clive Grinyer is an acknowledged expert in service design, design thinking, digital and technology innovation, and customer experience. He has led award-winning design teams for companies worldwide, including IDEO, and founded the consultancy Tangerine with Apple design chief Sir Jony Ive. He is a trustee of the Royal Society of Arts, a visiting professor at the Glasgow School of Art, and head of the pioneering service design program at the Royal College of Art in London.

The phenomenon of observational research is part of Clive's arsenal. He believes in building transdisciplinary teams to explore an audience's product and service experience, empathizing with them, and understanding their lives' patterns and flow. Through observation and direct experience, he fully explores an individual's journey to unlock unique insights to solve the problem.

"One of my favorite discovery stories was during the development process of Terminal 5 in Heathrow, London's major airport," says Clive. "As part of the future forecasting trend analysis work, the team identified that one particular trend was that people were aging quickly, yet were wealthy and healthy. Therefore, it was likely that older people would travel more. As part of the design research, they conducted extensive research of people around the airport to identify whether they could get some insight into the design process and make it human-centric to an older user. They immediately noticed that older people often went to the toilets, so an assumption was made that they obviously had weak bladders. They would have to increase the number of toilets in the terminal. However, one reluctant researcher was not convinced. They followed older people into the toilet and discovered they were standing around, listening to the announcements. That was the only place they could hear when their flight was called in a noisy airport that concentrated more on the retail environment than getting people to their gates."

HOW THE SOUL FOR MAKING ART WORKS

As a result, Terminal 5 now has multiple seating areas with robust sound systems and flight viewing signage, which has created a more relaxed experience.

"I love that epiphany of going into a toilet and finding somebody not doing what you would expect them to do and getting an insight that then drives your creativity to solve that problem," says Clive.

This unveiled two important themes of the creative process: the importance of looking left when others are looking right to seek the unseen by challenging the status quo, and that of rejecting the convention of what is perceived as the norm to find the best solution to the problem. You do not have to be an expert to solve a domain-specific problem. Being an "outsider", you can see a solution to the problem with an open mind and connect experiences and insights from multiple areas better than a domain specialist. They can sometimes get ingrained in their area and be part of the problem itself.

Thais Fonseca leads the brand strategy practice at the Brazilian-based creative agency Marcus com SAL. She specializes in turning strategic thinking and creativity into brand love – brought to life across a diverse Brazilian client portfolio, including Grupo Boticário, Beleaf, Beautybox, and Itaú.

"Everything begins with real research to frame the problem and understand the context, about the why, what, how, where, and when," she says. "Don't assume that you know everything. Keep an open mind, and conduct quantitative research on what can be measured, and qualitative research on the phenomenon, which can usually only be observed and described rather than measured. Once you dissect the research patterns, and insights emerge, then synthesize them into the right solution to the problem."

146

HOW THE
SOUL FOR
MAKING ART
WORKS

Thais continues, "I use an observational analysis technique where I deliberately go to the supermarket to look at the consumer products and how they are packaged and branded, the way people look, dress, and behave in shopping malls, what they buy and how, walking in the streets and getting the full sense of the community in cafés and restaurants, the food they eat, and the drinks they drink, which can be so quintessential and revealing to depicting consumer tastes and behaviors within a specific society and culture. I then infuse this within the research findings and solution design."

This research-led approach applies ethnographic and anthropological techniques and tools that encompass the observation of people's behavior in their natural situations to capture what they do. This approach helps understand cultural trends and lifestyle factors through context, norms, routine, and daily life habits within communities and societies. Ultimately informing organizations with the social context that influences their product creation and marketing process by informing the design, positioning, messaging, and packaging.

Maggie Hendrie is an interaction designer and founding chair of Art Center College of Design's Bachelor of Science in Interaction Design, and chairs their Graduate Media Design Practices MFA. "The first thing I do is observe to determine where there's a contradiction, gap, need, or story about a human experience that may not be evident," she says. "I try to find the paradox or contradiction that will inform the design intent. The move to a process includes observation, interviewing, contextual inquiry, diagramming, sketching, and prototyping."

HOW THE SOUL FOR MAKING ART WORKS

This technique is based on applying participatory design research to deeply understand the domain from multiple angles to uncover deeper context and meaning while challenging preconceptions and the status quo by answering questions that haven't been asked. Design begins by posing valuable questions: "If this could be done, what would it look like?", "Who is impacted, and what are the implications?" Then, one generating ideas by asking, "Imagine if...", "How could we...?". We need a tolerance for staying with the questions.

Craig Whittet is the Head of the Department for Product Design Engineering (PDE), a collaborative program taught at the Glasgow School of Art and the University of Glasgow. He educates, coaches, and mentors the next generation of product design engineers by blending creativity, design, and engineering science to create elegant, engaging experiences and products. The PDE program explores connections in everyday life by proactively anticipating and responding to culture, lifestyle, and industry trends. At its core, PDE is about applying technology to improve the quality of life. This is achieved through design, engineering, and commerce to make products related to human usage, behavior, and appeal.

"At a young age, I became fascinated by automotive design, the mechanics and how things were made and branded, their logo aesthetic and identity and how it can be replicated many times at scale, and how it all touched people through multiple touchpoints in different ways," says Craig. "Sketching is the point of origin in my creative process. I will sketch an idea from my imagination that may come from a feeling, vision, conversation, observation, and expression through drawing. Externalizing something that doesn't exist is still my key process of discovery and inventiveness. So, the appreciation of the mechanics of how things work and then having an opportunity to create ideas, concepts, and scenarios that don't actually exist still fascinates me to this day".

HOW THE SOUL FOR MAKING ART WORKS

This approach makes the invisible visible, seeing the unseen by lighting the way to the future by separating what is from what is not and transforming your imagination, dreams, and nascent ideas into reality, turning your daydreams into design!

Jason Milne was a retail designer in London for brands like Virgin, Tesco, and Marks & Spencer. He is an industry award winner for creativity, experience, and design effectiveness at Contagious, the Edinburgh-based creative brand agency, and a lecturer at Moonshine University in Kentucky. His work can be found in distilleries, brand homes, airports, and bars worldwide, including in Aberfeldy, Islay, Dublin, London, Louisville, Manhattan, and Texas. Jason has worked across multiple transdisciplinary brand-led experiential engagements in retail, media, education, beverages, and the hospitality industry. As part of Jason's human-centric design-based approach, he deliberately agitates the thought process in his quest for the best ideas by stretching his team's imagination to break preconceptions, habits, and stereotypes.

Jason says, "I will often encourage designers to think of the opposite of the right answer, something along the lines of 'what if this were a website?' when we are talking about a bottle, or suggesting a very contemporary finish in a traditional environment. Even asking people to think about what would be the most uncomfortable and awkward customer experience that one of our designs could create can help to free you from the shackles of first-good-idea-syndrome. This is because people can feel safe too quickly in the area they are working in. This can drive complacency and lazy thinking, so what I do is force them out of their comfort zones and routine and push them further into the unknown, which is why people actually do something exciting and break through."

HOW THE
SOUL FOR
MAKING ART
WORKS

Fred Warren is the founder of the design studio Wonder 14. He has worked with Donald Glover, Virgin Atlantic, Disney, Warner Brothers, L'Oreal, John Lewis, and Donald Glover to pioneer audience immersion experiences. "Creativity exists in all of us. It's in your heart and in your soul and not determined by what job you have. It is about tapping into your innate talent, experience, ability to empathize, and having the confidence to believe in your instincts." said Fred. "The creative process can be chaotic and messy, so free your imagination with childlike wonder and curiosity, and the persistence to navigate the unknown to craft a magical polyphony."

Mat Bancroft is an Art Director and Curator with a popular culture focus. Mat has been Johnny Marr's Art Director since 2012, was part of the curatorial team that organized and realized True Faith—an exhibition exploring the artistic legacy and influence of Joy Division and New Order at Manchester Art Gallery as part of Manchester International Festival in 2017. He's organized various pop culture archives, including the archives of Factory Records directors Tony Wilson and Rob Gretton, and his current work formalizing Derek Jarman's archive at Prospect Cottage for Art Fund UK. Mat's approach to the creative process is to fight for the artistic vision against the tensions that counter it by curating and detailing the movements he is inspired by and involved with by assembling, cataloging, managing, and presenting their artistic and cultural importance.

"It starts with the purpose and why we are doing this. How are we going to document that period? How far are we going to go into the catalog to define where we start and stop? What do we want the narrative and experience to be?" says Mat.

HOW THE SOUL FOR MAKING ART WORKS

"This involves going through a thorough process of being able to see around the corners by knowing where to search for and find the right information, understanding and identifying new and unexpected themes and sources, and discovering gems that separate the signal from the noise, then bringing order to the chaos by presenting the final curated output in a unified, consumable, insightful, and logical frame."

While studying for his degree at the Academy of Contemporary Music, Jonathan Burns envisioned and brought to life this innovative venture by reimagining the fashion industry's sustainability and reusability challenges ethically and respectfully. Jonathan is a fashion entrepreneur and the CEO of Stylecrate, which provides eco-friendly clothes delivered to your door every month.

He takes a holistic approach to his creative process by considering that his business and actions as an entrepreneur affect everyone in the industry. He also tries to be responsible for the impact that his business has on the world. He develops ideas by looking at all the areas and people they would touch from a moral standpoint, the perspective of what's going to happen, and the impact. He asks, "How can I reduce any negative impacts in so far as all the activities combined? By fostering a spontaneous idea, where an idea will kind of pop into your head, and you'll take it from there, and you will instinctively know what to do with it along the way." He continues, "You derive an idea after putting a lot of time and effort and thought into something, and it emerges from your work and becomes clearer and clearer."

From Budapest to Harvard, social media entrepreneur Csaba Dancshazy blazed a trail by building a social media analytic platform and practice at Microsoft, followed by an online consumer behavior platform at Wayfair.

HOW THE
SOUL FOR
MAKING ART
WORKS

Csaba then founded D-Tag Consulting to provide expertise, analytics, training, and custom consulting solutions that empower companies to build out and expand their return on investment (ROI) from social media analytics. Csaba's approach is based on convincing someone else of something valid. To do so, he follows a process. He says, "How do I prove that this has any kind of bearing on the real world? How do I know that this truly does represent what I think it represents? And so, there is yet another cycle of trial and error. If you're going to try something creative, anything creative, you're inevitably going to be going to places that you may not have expected. Being willing to go down that path as a part of the process is quite important. I obviously would never have gotten here had I sort of kept banging my head against the wall in the direction I originally took. So being adaptive and being willing to adjust is crucial."

Adam Farish is a musician, producer, sound engineer, and tech entrepreneur in a nationally touring Electronic Dance Music (EDM) band, and a DJ with two albums, multiple EPs, and several 12" singles to his credit. Adam is co-founder of SmartAmerica Home Automation and co-founder and CEO of 8Stem, a new audio format and platform that allows any listener to remix music on their phone. Adam feels that creativity is about having the ability to pivot and adjust thinking to fit the reality of what people want. He says, "Figuring out what to do next when you're forging into new territory and blazing new trails is crucial. Many times, you just don't know where to go because there are unlimited forks in the road, and some can be fruitful, while others can lead to your death."

Serial entrepreneur Spencer Stander has founded a charity that works with the fashion world to plant trees: Cool Green Fashion for Forests. He is a coveted artist with galleries in the Art District of downtown L.A., Laguna Beach, and Cape Cod exhibiting his

HOW THE SOUL FOR MAKING ART WORKS

his work. He has placed music in Warner Brothers features and network advertising campaigns, including during The Lord of The Rings network premiere. He holds two official selections with the John Lennon Songwriting Contest. He appeared on the History Channel as the "Dive Master" on Ancient Aliens. He has been employed by many television networks, covering a diverse range of jobs, including promotion, for which he holds eleven Gold Promax awards.

"Having a viable business is priority #1. No business means no art," says Spencer. "For the energy and input you put into the world, you get the same back. My creative process comes from doing things I love. Ideas find me, or I'll find them along my journey in the vein of the law of attraction, meaning what you put into the universe is what you get back. So, if you are constantly focused on debt, you're going to get more debt. If you're focused on creativity, you will get more creative, immediately or in the future. The key is to keep filling your artist's well. If your well is dry, you risk being creatively bankrupt and not coming up with new ideas and creating great work. Always take the time to proactively find inspiration from multiple sources to imagine new ideas to keep your well filled."

This approach is based on being business-smart and having a commercially viable value proposition, which generates income to fuel creativity, combined with doing good for the world by creating positive reactions, which produces new counteractions, and so on, which binds the living entity into karma. This creates memories, desires, and experiences, ultimately determining how you live your life by your actions.

After immersing himself in Shakespeare's language and craft at graduate school in Stratford-upon-Avon, Simon Leake joined Amazon.com in its second year of operation. He was part of the

HOW THE
SOUL FOR
MAKING ART
WORKS

team that built the company's customer service messaging. He then joined their editorial department to create content for the books and DVD divisions. After that, he became a freelance copywriter, creating video scripts for a wide variety of clients, including Microsoft, Nordstrom, HP, the World Bank, and the Gates Foundation.

He says, "I look for a voice, and I'm looking for a story. That story might be a very bare-bones kind of a narrative arc, a vague shape, or it might be something that feels more like a story. So, I'll be looking at the documents, the information, and the conversations I might have had with the client. Then, I try to sketch out vocabulary, narrative arcs, and things like that, then take that back to the client. Because often, at least at the beginning, what I find myself trying to do is get the client to work out what they want. It's a gathering of information, a distillation of that information to pick out the stuff that meets your purpose, and then a reinvention of that material. You have to keep your ego in check because you've got to be able to throw things away that you may think are great."

Product innovator and business executive Gary Burt is an eclectic and visionary thought leader who has guided the success of multiple breakthrough products and services at technology companies: Microsoft, O2, Siemens, Atos, and Blue Prism. He has set the strategy, roadmap, and feature definition to maximize business value by being deeply committed and continuously honing his craft. He does this through quality execution and completeness of the entire product life cycle with a focus on the design-based, human-centered approach.

"Making the invisible visible is about making your products and services relate to people," said Gary. "This is the acid test that will save you a fortune in resources and time. If people don't

HOW THE
SOUL FOR
MAKING ART
WORKS

care, then stop doing it, because this is why we see so many products fail. Go back one, two, three, or however many steps it takes, and rapidly iterate until the point where you can make your product something that people need and get a meaningful experience from. Don't waste time and energy trying to use market research data and subjective interpretations to show that what you've done is worthy. Make the emotional and human connection first and foremost. That is what makes the invisible visible. If not, go back, reset, pivot, and restart!"

This is based upon years of guiding the success of multiple breakthrough products and services at technology companies. Including your target consumers and infusing their perspective into all steps of the problem-solving process by understanding the problem, designing the right solution, then implementing it.

"It is not about technology. It's about the people. Great product design is about enabling people to improve and enrich their lives. That's how big your goal needs to be. It doesn't matter whether it is a Swiss Army knife, a Rolex, an iPhone, or a Tesla. The fundamentals are the same: improve the human experience with your product. That's it!" says Gary. "Don't be fooled into thinking that it is a technology manifesto, because it isn't. It's about using technology as an enabler to make beautiful products of use to a human's life in a way that surprises and delights. The elegantly weighted sharp knife that's a delight to use, that stays sharp, and is a joy to hold. An oven that is easy to program and doesn't overcook your food. A car that is safer to drive but is also fun. Design for people by creating unforgettable experiences that improve their lives and have a meaningful impact on society."

7 LEADING WITHOUT FRONTIERS

LEADING
WITHOUT
FRONTIERS

The creative leadership values, principles, and competencies. The five learning stages and personas of creative leadership: Fledgling, Journeyman, Expert, Innovator, and Artist. The behaviors, knowledge, skills, and proficiencies to build creative competency in your team and organization, and the manifesto for creating without frontiers that arms your arsenal to achieve creative freedom and excellence.

LEADING
WITHOUT
FRONTIERS

Leading without frontiers means creative leadership that encompasses disruptive thinking and practice to drive radical improvements in their respective domain, discipline, and industry. It means reaching the other side by leading toward new frontiers of unknown opportunities, unfulfilled hopes, and dreams by doing things your own way and in your own style, with the taste and grace needed to find the way forward for a better life and society.

Award-winning inventor and engineer Bob Stephen co-founded Equalizer International Ltd to design and develop a range of cost-saving industrial tools which were adopted throughout the Oil and Gas, Mining and Renewable Energy sectors. The products went on to become recognized as Industry best-practice methods reducing risk to personnel.

"When trying to find a solution to a problem, my creative process is like a tombola machine. I introduce the problem, switch it on, and the ideas generate randomly; some are discarded immediately, some put aside for consideration at a later stage, and others captured immediately for further analysis," says Bob. "Once the problem is stored in the machine, the process can be turned on and off whenever I want. Sometimes the ideas become tiring and irrelevant, then I switch the process off. The process can take time and often starts when I least expect, then before I know, it's generating real, relevant ideas and solutions in overdrive. The Eureka moment is realizing I've hit the Jackpot with a winner by making it real."

CREATIVE
LEADERS

Creativity is the most distinguishable quality for every leader in every domain. Creative leaders display distinctly different behaviors, values, and characteristics from traditional management, and they get exponential results, inspire creativity in others, build productive teams, and drive successful businesses. Yet while many organizations claim that they value creative leadership, most of them pay lip service to the idea to rev up the past by promoting leaders who do not espouse creative leadership, and instead are perceived as safer, risk-averse, and more likely to maintain the status quo, which is diametrically opposed to the necessary leadership needed to move the world forward.

Creative leaders possess a distinctly engaging and inspirational leadership style because they truly put people first, are perceptive about their needs, are inclusive of and empathetic toward different cultures, promote diversity and difference, and have a purpose-led mission-driven approach to making people's lives better and advancing society toward the greater good. They hold themselves accountable for their actions and have a social conscience and empathy for the environment by continuously managing innovation that powers the products they design, make, and sell, and the businesses they run.

They have the intuition, skills, and ability to see the unseen and make the invisible visible by lighting the way to the future and separating what is from what is not. They connect past and present to create something new. They manifest what is inside and around them in everyday life, transcending the ordinary and routine into something that has societal value by putting things together in a way that has never been done before.

CREATIVE LEADERS

Creative leaders have confidence in their ideas, and never give up on bringing them to fruition! It means leading without frontiers by seeing around the corners and fearlessly navigating into the future. They inspire, empower, and stimulate people and teams to achieve the unexpected and exceed normal performance levels. They have the charisma that engages and excites and inspires and motivates people by having and living a compelling vision that provides clarity, generates enthusiasm, and delivers success, always! They are genuinely empathetic toward people's needs and feelings, and help them grow and become self-actualized, which, along with their transparency and honesty, solidifies trust and confidence in them.

Purpose, autonomy, and mastery are what people need to optimize their creativity. You need to think with your own mind, feel with your own heart, and create with your own hands. Strive for simplicity to remove inefficiency, never to complicate. Design for people, not machines. Know what technology can enable and that there are times and places where technology is not the right answer. Love paper, pen, and whiteboards because they are a blank canvas, which is the most powerful tool. Seek freedom, not compliance, and respect standards, but thrive by breaking the rules to find and realize the best solution to the problem. Invent, make mistakes, improve, seek excellence, and reject conformity and mediocrity.

CREATIVE
LEADERS

Marie Curie discovered radium and polonium and their contribution to finding cancer treatments. Polymath Leonardo DaVinci created early designs and drawings for flying machines, human anatomy, and the first robot in recorded history. Henry Ford changed how people lived and moved around by making cars affordable to the everyday person. The common thread is that they were all driven by a people-first approach, where the ultimate outcome of what they produced advanced humanity's well-being. They are prime examples of creative leaders in their times and fields because they did things differently, rejecting failure and swimming against the tide of adversity to break through the frontiers to provide novel solutions to complex problems we didn't know existed. They disrupted existing industries and created brand new worlds that became the norm.

"My style is completely instinctive," said the artist, Anita Kunz. "When you look at my work, it is drawn fairly incorrectly because I didn't actually have an art education that was about art, not illustration, nor did I learn any art history. My eyes were wide open as far as influences go because I knew nothing about anything. I was simply drawing from what was inside my head, then using photographic or any physical references, which developed into a style from years of drawing practice. It's never good to try to mimic or manufacture a style, because it needs to be authentic and develop naturally."

Dream up what doesn't exist, and turn your imagination into art. This is similar to outsider art, where there is an innocent quality in people who have not been trained as artists or worked within the conventional art production structures because they do not follow a conventional path, structure, or formula.

CREATIVE
LEADERS

The learnings for finding creative success are to; "Work hard. Put in the hours, and you'll get better. It's a process; it's a journey, so don't be too hard on yourself," says Anita. "Embrace self-doubt. It will propel you forward. Remove toxic influences. Surround yourself with excellence. Nurture your uniqueness. It is important to be uniquely yourself; it's what the best artists have done. Not working can be just as important to creativity as working. Go for a run, watch a movie, take a nap. Neuroscience confirms that sometimes the brain has to completely disengage to come up with a good idea. Be kind and stay humble. To quote Kurt Vonnegut: 'There's only one rule that I know of, babies—God damn it, you've got to be kind.' Contribute where you can. Take care of yourself! Try not to use materials that hurt you or the environment. Fixative, turpentine, try not to use them or use proper ventilation if you have to. Remain a student for life and stay curious and open-minded. Always be learning, whatever form it takes, and stop trying to be perfect! Learn, ask tons of questions, and absorb information like a sponge!"

CREATIVE
LEADERS

CREATION IS NOT IMITATION

Many influential artists, designers, musicians, filmmakers, actors, writers, poets, entrepreneurs, industrialists, and technologists started as imitators of their craft's current greats. Still, once they found their voice and sound, they became unstoppable in their own right. They are innovators who broke the bonds of their era to create high art, and their own original experience cultivated a movement for change.

Take The Beatles, for example. They started off imitating American Gospel, R&B, rockabilly, and early rock 'n' roll as fledglings. Their music dealt with love songs and teen relationships, which was the standard fare of the day. They became journeymen until they mastered their technical expertise as musicians and songwriting experts. Similarly, to artists like; Banksy, Dali, Matisse, Michelangelo, Picasso, and Andy Warhol, who started off as imitators of the masters of that time to learn and develop their craft until they found their style. About halfway through their duration, they found their authentic voice and style and produced lyrics and music about everyday life and observations in their native Liverpudlian accents. Ultimately, they became artists who revolutionized how music was made and acted as a catalyst and soundtrack for social justice movements. Albums such as *Sergeant Pepper's Lonely Hearts Club Band* provided one of the most potent musical cornerstones to the now legendary "summer of love". The Beatles have maintained a canonized status unprecedented for musicians to date.

Expertise is not enough to change the world in any field and discipline. Innovation and artistry require the ability to transcend time and create a culture and movement manifested through your own unique identity, aesthetics, and the world around you.

CREATIVE LEADERS

"Think of yourself as an Artist, first and foremost. Do what you do from an authentic place within yourself," said musician and producer, Martyn Ware.

Fiorenza Plinio is the Head of Creative Excellence at the Cannes Lions International Festival of Creativity, where she nurtures creativity across all the company's products and services and creates continuous innovation and engagement with the global creative community and organizations, building programs that bring to life the highest levels of creativity at the largest gathering of the advertising and creative communications industry and beyond.

"There are two dimensions when it comes to evaluating creative excellence: business impact and social good," says Fiorenza. "It is not about being creative for creativity's sake. It is about being creative and producing something new and different that can also impact ROI. However, it also has to be about creating something that has true value, that improves people's lives and helps progress society by putting purpose and ethics at the center and being responsible for addressing some of the world's issues, such as global warming and sustainability." Fiorenza continued, "This is how you measure creative excellence. I believe that the best work that usually wins awards is about applying creativity to positively impact society by being inclusive and socially responsible and by putting ethics at the center of the creative intent and of what businesses stand for."

"I had an insatiable curiosity for how things were made and worked from a young age, such as; cars and motorbikes. As a baby boomer growing up in the 1960s and 1970s working-class Scotland, I didn't have much, forcing me to be resourceful by making my own entertainment, like building wooden Go Karts from abandoned prams and discarded wood, with a hammer and nails for tools to put it together. For me, this was creativity at its

CREATIVE
LEADERS

finest, and in hindsight, the origins of my apprenticeship for a lifelong journey of designing and making products that solved real-life problems to make people's lives easier," said the engineer, Bob Stephen.

"Creativity exists within everyone, yet can be overlooked within our everyday routine. From art to music, design to dance, mathematics to science, we develop new ideas and solutions to things that didn't exist previously. We call it progress. We all have hidden talents and the ability to be creative, and it needs nurturing to shine through than locked inside ourselves. Sometimes we develop a novel idea that excites us, enlightening our minds to wonder enthusiastically by navigating through a thought process of possibility and hope. To then be countered by our pragmatic instincts, which can fuel self-doubt; "What if?" and "Don't be silly!" by discarding these ideas and reverting to the status quo."

The key is to make a living from doing what you love. Your life journey will be naturally littered with enriched experiences, self-fulfillment, and happiness by following your passion. Ignore the crowd and work to develop a deeper relationship between your inner self and your purpose in life, and follow it with instinct and mission by being authentic. Lead with conviction and confidence, and stay true to yourself.

What is required to take the leap from expert to artistic innovator? A true artist is at the summit of what a human can aspire to and achieve in their respective domain.

CREATIVE EXCELLENCE MODEL

The Creative Excellence Model is a guide to help creative leaders, teams, and organizations build sustainable creative capability. Grounded in real patterns and insights gleaned from some of the most creative teams and organizations globally, it formalizes behaviors from a cluster of knowledge, skills, abilities, and motivations. It prescribes the desired performance patterns required by diagnosing and evaluating performance and talent.

BEHAVIORS, KNOWLEDGE & SKILLS

	LEADERSHIP	AESTHETICS & IDENTITY	INDUSTRY & CULTURE	CRAFTSMANSHIP
5 ARTIST	Leads through artistry and personal mastery towards invisible horizons by lighting the way into the future	Leads through artisty and personal mastery to create aesthetic vision and identity	Leads through artistry and personal mastery of creative outputs in context of industry and culture.	Leads through artisty and personal mastery through excellence of craft.
4 INNOVATOR	Innovates through breakthrough execution towards invisible horizons	Innovates through breakthrough execution of aesthetic vision and identity	Innovates through breakthrough execution of creative outputs in context of the industry	Innovates through breakthrough execution excellence of craft.
3 EXPERT	Guides through domain expertise towards invisible horizons	Guides through domain expertise of aesthetic vision and identity	Guides through domain expertise of creative outputs in context of the industry	Guides through domain expertise of craft
2 JOURNEYMAN	Applies insight and contributes independently towards invisible horizons	Applies insights and contributes independently to aesthetic vision and identity	Applies insights and contributes independently to creative outputs in context of the industry	Applies insights and contributes independently to develop craft
1 FLEDGLING	Acquires knowledge and know-how to develop towards invisible horizons	Acquires knowledge and know-how of aesthetic vision and identity	Acquires knowledge and know-how of creative outputs in context of the industry	Acquires knowledge and know-how of craft

Left axis (bottom to top): DISCOVERY, INVENTION, INNOVATION (PROFICIENCY)
Right progression: PROFICIENCY, INNOVATION

CREATIVE EXCELLENCE MODEL

There are five learning stages of creative leadership: Fledgling, Journeyman, Expert, Innovator, and Artist; there are also four distinct behaviors, knowledge, and skill clusters: leadership, aesthetics and identity, industry, and cultural insights craftsmanship. These make use of three proficiencies: discovery, invention, and innovation.

One of our most fundamental life needs is to create, next to air, water, food, shelter, safety, sleep, clothing, and belonging. Creativity is a core discipline, like reading, writing, and arithmetic. It is not incidental and nice to have. Rather, it is a way of life.

The Creative Excellence Model is a collection of skills and competencies identified as necessary for success in creative leadership positions. It comprises a set of principles defining what creative leaders must know and do. It incorporates practices essential for all levels, from Fledgling to Expert to Innovator to Artist. It holistically addresses leadership at the individual, team, and organizational levels.

It contains definitions and examples of each competency, particularly where it deals with different performance levels for each of the expected behaviors that contribute to advancement. Using a competency-based approach to leadership, organizations and teams can better determine and grow their next generation of creative leaders by instilling which behaviors, values, skills, and competencies are required, valued, recognized, and rewarded in their performance management systems.

CREATIVE
EXCELLENCE
MODEL

The five learning stages require a balance of people at each level, with a majority at the expert stage. People will move through the stages in different times throughout their careers.

The five stages are:

1. FLEDGLING Acquiring knowledge and know-how.
2. JOURNEYMAN Applying insight and contributing independently.
3. EXPERT Guiding through domain expertise.
4. INNOVATOR Innovating through breakthrough execution.
5. ARTIST Leading through artistry and personal mastery.

People have the distinct option to develop a breadth of disciplines across multiple industries, businesses, and technical areas or develop depth in more focused disciplines in a specific industry, business, and technical area.

People at the Expert, Innovator, and Artist stages perform differently (not necessarily more or better) than those at Fledgling or Journeyman stages, as leadership, interpersonal, and strategic skills become more relevant. The process is not necessarily completely cyclical either. Typically, you will always start as a fledgling when something is new to you or if the environment or technology has changed. You then progress to journeyman as you become able to operate independently. Learning is a social process and involves peripheral activities, where people take on more complex activities as they grow in confidence and see their peers perform them.

The learning never stops!

CREATIVE
EXCELLENCE
MODEL

You may then choose to stay at the Journeyman level as you go "deep" in this competency, for example, if you become a subject-matter expert. Or you may move on because you become a team leader or a mentor in that competency area, rather than journeying yourself. You start to help and guide others on how to journey effectively. This requires slightly different personal skills and qualities, as you need to lead and teach people.

People at the Expert and Innovator levels are typically leading a movement and complex novel pursuit, engagement, or project in a particular area to break new ground and set a new direction. Effective leadership behaviors do, therefore, become very important as you reach these stages.

5 Artist
Leading through artistry and personal mastery

4 Innovator
Innovating through breakthrough execution

3 Expert
Guiding through domain expertise

2 Journeyman
Applying insight and contributing independently

1 Fledgling
Acquiring knowledge and know-how

Proficiency

Creativity, invention, and innovation are intrinsically linked and essential for growth and mastery.

Developing creative ideas and concepts by translating them into purposeful action.

DISCOVERY

The creation of novel solutions that have not been discovered previously.

INVENTION

Turning new concepts that have value into commercial success for widespread use.

INNOVATION

The ability to conceive of something original or unusual and turn it into reality.

CREATION

Leadership

Lead towards invisible horizons with fearless expression, connecting to emotions and imagination that fuel consistent action, evoking wonder and magic to create the future.

CREATIVITY

Generate novel ideas that have value, and inspire energy, enthusiasm, and action.

VISION

Formulate and articulate a clear vision and direction that synthesizes the unknown into the known.

AGILITY

Adapt to and navigate through adversity and change with curiosity and persistence.

RESULTS

Authentically generate energy through passion and engagement by cultivating a movement that drives successful outcomes with positive impact.

Aesthetics and identity

Blend the art and science of aesthetics to create engaging outcomes.

Design and direct the aesthetic vision to enable product creation that connects emotionally and delivers value to audiences.

AESTHETIC CREATION

Define guidance to set expected standards that infuse through the entire branded assets and experiences.

CREATIVE PRINCIPLES

Establish and articulate creative direction to drive brand cohesion and integrity across all touchpoints.

BRAND COHESION

Take a data-driven approach to inform direction, messaging, and positioning by leveraging qualitative and quantitative research methods.

RESEARCH & POSITIONING

Industry and cultural insights

Proactively respond to the forces at work that drive change to the creation of products, services, or experiences.

TREND SETTING

Anticipate opportunities to set future trends based on sociocultural, economic, political, and technological drivers.

SYNTHESISES

Infuse the relevance of market trends to new solutions and future direction and set the strategy for timing, design, and positioning for the future.

NURTURE

Develop or acquire talent with specific skills and expertise to realize the desired vision.

MARKET RESEARCH & ANALYSIS

Understand market needs and create new products and services to address audience needs.

Craftsman-ship

Continuously improve craft through constant skills honing, acquiring new experiences to remain relevant and innovative, and maintaining quality focus to the last detail.

TECHNICAL EXCELLENCE

Ensure technical depth and breadth in domain to remain relevant and innovative.

INNOVATION

Progressively improve creative outputs by working across multiple disciplines to ensure longevity and optimal impact.

ROLE MODEL

Commit to creative advancement, inspiring and guiding others to deliver innovative outputs.

FUTURING

Anticipate the future and adapt to change throughout time.

Behaviors

Always be future-oriented. A Dreamer, Maker, and Doer who starts and moves things forward with a bias for action, and inspiring others to do it.

ADAPTABILITY

Adapt to change and navigate throug ambiguity, curiosity, and persistence.

COLLABORATION

Cross pollinate across multiple domains to seek inspiration and expertise to force multiple innovative outcomes.

AUDIENCE FOCUSED

Intuitively anticipate audience needs and proactively provide solutions that surprise and delight.

BIAS FOR ACTION

Activate transformative change with persistence and resilience to stay the course.

The
FLEDGLING

A Fledgling learns how to do a specialized job through curiosity in a domain combined with a willingness to learn their craft through on-the-job training, coaching, mentoring, and acquiring the practical know-how. Understanding and applying creative principles, frameworks, techniques, and tools to develop their expertise by expanding their knowledge and skills. They take on responsibility through initiative, self-motivation, problem solving, adaptability, and teamwork, which evolves through commitment, perseverance, creative energy, and enthusiasm.

The
JOURNEYMAN

A Journeyman is a maker and doer, skilled in a given craft. A lifelong learner and adventurer, driven by insatiable intellectual curiosity, a Journeyman makes their thirst for knowledge and experiential skill development a continuous pursuit. Ever the student, they experience the world as an endless opportunity for learning and discovery by expanding their knowledge (often into disparate topics), experimenting, tinkering, and deepening their subject-matter expertise with a bias for action.

The
EXPERT

The Expert is a master craftsman who has specialist skills and expertise in their specific domain. They are skilled and adept in their craft after spending years perfecting it. Dedicated to their craft and in constant pursuit of personal mastery, they take creative risks, find joy and play in the process, are critical thinkers, and ask the big questions.

They are intellectually curious, can find and create meaning, are driven by tangible results, and know how to deliver and play the long game, and understand the hard work that goes into building something of value over time. Experts' natural gift is focus and dedication. They seek to achieve personal mastery and be perceived as authorities and role models in their field.

The
INNOVATOR

The Innovator is a pioneer and risk-taker with an insatiable curiosity to light the way into the future, which no one has charted. They break through the status quo to find new horizons by moving, shaking, and disrupting the world by mastering the art and science of conjuring up and bringing ideas to life. They guide the rest of us to learn, adapt, and thrive in transformative change by generating compelling solutions, tap into their inner grit and persistence, and stay the course.

The
ARTIST

The Artist has a holistic global view and sees the world as it should be. Charismatic and self-expressive, they inspire and excite, helping people visualize the way forward, and create and compel a community and movement with shared values and ideals to follow suit. Their superpower is to make the invisible visible and create a whole new world around that, leading people toward an invisible horizon. They are fearless in their expression, transcend the status quo, and stand against the convention and naysayers.

LEARNING WITHOUT FRONTIERS

Learning is critical to human existence. As water and food nourish our bodies, so too do information and knowledge fuel our minds. Acquiring critical and creative thinking skills, communication skills, and the ability to collaborate is key to our self-growth and leading a fulfilling life.

Learning is a social process. We grow in confidence by observing how others perform and excel. People have different learning styles and preferences, which take on various forms instead of fitting into one specific pattern. It is essential to be aware and adaptive within the learning process to minimize exclusion and optimize for the best learning experience and outcome.

"Be open, determined, and willing to really push yourself and explore who you are as a person," said Cherry Valentine, performance artist who grew up within a Roma Gypsy community in the North East of England, which fueled Cherry's creative instincts, a bias for adventure, and freedom for expression, to emerge as an influential voice in the Lesbian, Gay, Bisexual, and Transgender (LGBT+) community by combining life experience, curiosity, comedy, and satire into performance art.

The point is that everyone is capable of learning, and that parents, brothers, sisters, friends, teachers, coaches, managers, and leaders—anyone and everyone—is influencing a person's learning journey. The key is to understand and adapt to different learning styles, especially in the earlier years of learning, which can have an enormous impact on an individual's ability to learn and empower themselves for their future, to live a happy and fulfilled life by gaining positive experiences along the way.

Attitude
Imagination Execution

The five principles for how to create without frontiers are:

Manifesto

1   **KNOW THAT RIDICULE IS NOTHING TO BE AFRAID OF**
If your efforts are met with ridicule, all you have to do is find your inner conviction that you are doing the right thing, navigating toward invisible horizons by anticipating future trends inspired by culture and aesthetics to drive sustained discovery, invention, and innovation. It's a sure sign that what you do is bold and innovative if you're dancing to your own drumbeat. Pay no mind to ridicule.

2   **NEVER BE "ANOTHER BRICK IN THE WALL"**
Dream, make and do. Be in the moment. Push forward for the greater good with true grit. Conformity never leads to progress. If you have something authentically different to offer, you'll excite and inspire others and ultimately thrive by lighting the way to the future.

3   **LEAD WITHOUT FRONTIERS**
Fearlessly lead by example and win the crowd by navigating territory where no one else has ventured. Avoid the mainstream and work to develop a deeper relationship between yourself and your audience. Be authentic, live in the moment with conviction and confidence, and always stay true to yourself.

4   **PROKOVE ACTIONS THAT CHANGES MINDS**
Reject conventions, constantly analyze, and question and challenge the status quo in your everyday life. Provide an alternative and bring it to life. People who achieve greatness do not fit a formula or follow a structure. They break the mold by following their own path.

5   **KEEP TRUE TO THE DREAMS OF YOUR YOUTH AND CREATE OUTSIDE THE BOUNDARIES**
Pablo Picasso believed all children are artists, but they lose their creativity when they grow up. Grow into, not out of, creativity. Don't give up the dreams of your childhood and your approach to the world through a child's eyes. Learn, innovate, and never waste a second on anything that seems to restrict you.

DON'T LET
THE FUTURE LEAVE YOU BEHIND

Follow your heart and do what you love by falling in love with your craft, pursue it with intensity, and be exceptional at it. Everything you need is already inside of you. Free yourself from others' expectations and walk away from the games and boundaries they impose upon you. Only you know your true worth!

Realizing your full potential to live a fulfilled life means unlocking and applying your creative potential to do and excel at what you love.

Remember, our outputs are the next generation's inputs! That comes with accountability and responsibility to pass the baton to the next generation by leaving the world in better shape than you found it. Make it count!

It is all about attitude, imagination, and execution.

ABOUT THE
AUTHOR

Roy Sharples is the Founder and Chief Executive Officer of Unknown Origins. Roy is on a mission to unlock everyone's creative potential. An entrepreneur, artist, and maker at the intersection of creativity and commerciality - with eclectic experience at building beloved brands, bringing new products and services to market, creating growth businesses at scale, and start-ups from the ground up.

AT THE
HELM

Narrative and Creative Direction: Roy Sharples

Design: Devon Baker

Design Execution: David Prendergast

Editorial: Jo Finchen-Parsons and Simon Leake

Contribution: Gary Burt co-wrote
"Utopian Futures: A World Rebooted"

Sources: Unless where stated, all quotations
referenced from interviews captured within the
Unknown Origins podcast, blog series, or electronic
mail and granted with kind permission to use within
this book by each interviewee.

https://www.unknownorigins.com/podcast
https://www.unknownorigins.com/blog

WITHOUT
WHOM

Paula, Lucas, Indiana, and Archie.

THANK
YOU

Creativity Without Frontiers
How to make the invisible visible by lighting the way into the future.

Paperback ISBN: 978-1-7365686-0-6
Hardback ISBN: 978-1-7365686-1-3
Ebook ISBN: 978-1-7365686-2-0

For more information: info@unknownorigins.com
www.unknownorigins.com

INDEX

Unknown Origins

Made in the USA
Middletown, DE
05 September 2021